UNZIPPED

A Toolkit for Life

Matt Whyman

*Hodder
Children's
Books*

A division of Hachette Children's Books

**Medical Consultant
Dr Dan Rutherford**

Illustrations by

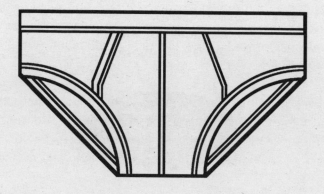

I'd like to thank the following for their support, help and encouragement in getting this book into your hands: Anne Clark; Margaret Conroy, Naomi Pottesman and all at Hodder Children's Books; Chris, Lawrence, Lester, Philip, Shamsul and Thabo of Pimlico School; and everyone at DGA.

about matt whyman

Matt Whyman is best known as a popular magazine agony uncle and as a frank spokesman on teen and relationship issues. He has written numerous health awareness campaigns, for Radio One, the Health Education Authority and Brook Advisory.

Matt is part of the award-winning team at TheSite.org, the UK's leading online resource for young people. He is also the author of several novels and three Wise Guides for teenagers on the subject of divorce, smoking and drinking.

Text copyright © Matt Whyman 2002, 2007
Illustrations copyright © Kerb 2002

Book design by Don Martin

First published in 2002 as XY – A TOOLKIT FOR LIFE
This updated edition published in Great Britain in 2007
by Hodder Children's Books

The right of Matt Whyman to be identified as the
author of this Work and of Kerb as the
illustrator of this Work has been asserted by them in
accordance with the Copyright, Designs and Patents Act 1988.

A catalogue record for this book is available
from the British Library.

ISBN-13: 978 0 340 94533 9

Printed in the UK by CPI Bookmarque, Croydon, CR0 4TD

Hodder Children's Books
A division of Hachette Children's Books
338 Euston Road, London NW1 3BH
An Hachette Livre UK company

contents

being a boy

Right now, there's a lot to be said for being young and male. It's a laugh, for a start. Together with your mates, you learn stuff like how to perform a Chinese burn to maximum effect, the best way to spit so it doesn't dribble down your chin, or talk about football like you personally invented the game. There are always dares to be made, jokes to be told, or wisecracks to be had at someone else's expense, and let's not even start on the subject of drink and drugs or girls and sex ...

Living life as a lad has all the makings of one long party, but you know deep down there's a lot more going on – the anxiety that comes with wondering if you're the only one who doesn't exactly know what a blow job is, for example, or the fear that friends might discover you can't sleep at night because you're worried about exams. In short, we're talking about all the things we don't feel able to express, because, well, that's how it is for boys.

Which is where **Unzipped** comes in. How? By unleashing all the facts, strategies and advice you need to feel confident in yourself.

Nowadays it can seem as if everyone is down on boys, and that somehow if we were more like girls the world would be a better place. Unzipped doesn't go there. You won't find any kind of judgement about who you are or what you're like, or attempt to spin you some kind of agenda. It just serves up clear and balanced info about issues central to your life, and leaves the smart moves up to you.

From here on out, you'll get a run down of the physical changes that kick in with puberty, even tips on shaving and sorting out spots. We'll look at your willy, too – not literally, but you'll find everything you need to know about good tackle management but never dared ask. From sex to sexuality, drink and drugs, to dealing with friends, family and even your mindset, here's a handbook that's packed with everything you need to make informed decisions and really start living your life as it should be – free from worry and with everything to play for!

1. what makes a man?

"I heard you go through physical changes during puberty. At first I thought my shirt would rip apart and make way for huge muscles!"
Jamie, 11

"I wish I was able to grow a goatee beard, but I have a feeling it's not going to happen for me in a big way. I can barely get a stubbly chin."
Chris, 14

"I'm fed up with being thought of as a boy. I just want to be like everyone else."
Kaj, 13

A PEEK UNDER THE BONNET

It's a shame we aren't born with an instruction manual – one written especially for each of us that gives the lowdown on puberty and the changes it brings. That way, we'd have a reliable source of info we could turn to whenever we needed some answers. It has to beat just motoring along and hoping that everything's functioning properly, or waiting until something breaks down before asking for help.

The reality is that lads grow up lacking a lot of vital knowledge about their developing bodies, and find it hard to open up about stuff they need to take on board. For example, if we had periods – like girls – things might be a bit different. It might encourage your dad to sit down with you at some point and discuss the changes you face in adolescence. He would want to make sure that you felt prepared, and that you were comfortable about coming to him with any questions you had.

Another problem is the fact that boys tend to grow up in a competitive environment, so it's easy to fret when your mate makes a big noise about the fact that his voice has broken and you're still squeaking like a choirboy. As a result, we're quick to create the impression that everything is dangling as it should, and claim that we could grow a beard if we really wanted to, but we just can't be bothered, OK?

In a couple of years, with all the changes behind you, you and your mates will realise that dick size or chest hair is no measure of a man. Until then, here are the edited highlights of that manual we never had.

Puberty primer

● *Puberty is the term given to a stage in which your body develops at a rapid rate, turning you from boy to man.*

- *You may get taller, broader, hairier, spotty and sweatier too. More about this on pages 6–15.*

- *Your voice deepens, your balls drop and your knob appears to take on a life of its own. Read all about it on pages 16–26.*

- *'Growing pains' may kick in occasionally – brief but sudden twinges in your back, legs or arms. Believed to be part of the puberty process, but always get checked out by your doctor if you're worried, or if the pain nags for a while.*

- *The hormones responsible for these changes kick in any time between 10 and 18.*

- *Girls tend to be the first to go through growth spurts, though boys soon catch up, and often wind up taller.*

- *Puberty lasts for several years, but the rate you mature won't make any difference to the finished result.*

Standing proud

Ultimately, we're all built in the same way and the changes stop when you're fully developed. Until then, however, it's all too easy to feel shy about the shape your body's taking, or watch other lads grow bigger or more brawny and worry that you're being left behind. The trouble with any kind of comparison is that it breeds insecurity and can knock your self-confidence. What's more, measuring up really doesn't make a man. That comes from understanding what's going on with your own mind and body, while being happy and at home with yourself.

2. surface stuff

"I know lads suffer from spots just as much as girls, but it's easier for them to buy stuff from the chemist. Guys can't be seen to fuss with creams and lotions. Not in public, at any rate!"
Tom, 15

"During puberty, I would often start sweating for no apparent reason."
Saul, 16

"When my voice was breaking, I hated talking to girls in case I opened my mouth and a squeak came out!"
Neil, 15

SPOTS

The hormones responsible for puberty act a little bit like electricity. When they start to swirl around the bloodstream, we get switched on to all things passionate and lusty. The downside is that hormones can also wire us up with spots. How? By stimulating production of natural oil in the skin called sebum. This gets secreted onto the surface through tiny open pores. A spot crops up when pores clog with oil and skin debris. Bacteria then set to work, inflaming the area and creating anything from blackheads to pimples and cysts.

"I used to feel shy about spots, but then I got fed up with it ruling my life."
Jon, 15

Fast facts

- *Nearly 70% of all lads get spots, or acne. Not just on the face but the back, neck, shoulders and chest.*

- *It's a cruel myth that people with spots are dirty. In general, people with acne keep their skin cleaner than most.*

- *Research shows that for the majority of acne sufferers, diet has no bearing whatsoever on the condition.*

- *And before you ask, there is no evidence to suggest that sex affects spots either!*

Standing up to spots

Nobody likes getting spots. They can make you feel badly self-conscious, especially if it's your face that's affected. But having acne that everyone can see is often the best way of dealing with it. Why? Because when it's out in the open you have nothing to hide. You may feel embarrassed around people to begin with, but you'll soon realise that they're far more interested in the kind of person you are inside.

Keep it clean

Getting into a washing routine will help keep things under control, but don't go mad. Wash your face no more than twice a day, or risk over-stimulating the oil in the skin.

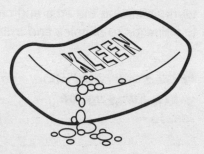

Be sussed about soap

Many standard soaps have a drying effect, and this actually increases the chances of clogged pores and spots. Your best bet is to sample the range of over-the-counter skin care products available at the chemist. Skin experts recommend products containing benzoyl peroxide – always read the application instructions carefully.

Look after your towel

Leave your towel in a heap on the bathroom floor and, next time you dry off, you're effectively smearing bacteria over your skin. Use a clean towel as often as possible, and let it dry out thoroughly between uses.

Sun sense

Sunlight can play a part in treating acne by encouraging the skin to peel and drying up excess grease. However, there's a limit to how much sun the skin can take before you end up doing more harm than good. Think moderation, and use a sunscreen in milk or cream form (as opposed to oil), so as not to clog pores. Also be sure to check the SPF (sun protection factor) and go for nothing less than SPF15 to help block the sun's harmful UV rays.

Face your doctor

Don't be afraid of going to your doctor about spots. He or she can provide specific antibiotic lotions and tablets that work effectively by slowing the build up of bacteria which cause spots. (More information about dealing with your doc on pages 35–36.)

For advice, support and information of dealing with spots, contact the Acne Support Group on 0870 870 2263.

UNZIPPED INFORMER

Q: What happens when my voice 'breaks'?
Rachid, 14

A: Don't worry, nothing actually gets broken! You're talking about a stage during puberty in which your voice deepens in tone. It's all down to the increase in testosterone surging round your system, which causes the voice box (larynx) to grow. Some lads barely notice the change, while others may experience a slightly dry throat for a few weeks, plus a tendency for their voice to squeak unpredictably!

BODY HAIR

Our relationship with body hair is weird. Girls go to great lengths to get rid of theirs, spending time and money on waxing and plucking, bleaching and shaving, while many guys regard hair as a sign of macho maturity and wish they could be more gorilla-like.

"I started shaving long before I actually needed to. Nowadays, I have to shave every day and the fact is it's a bit of a pain!"
Eddie, 19

Body hair is one of the most visible signs that puberty is underway, and results in hair sprouting from your armpits and legs, around your goolies and possibly even on your chest too. Facial hair is an even bigger deal, because it's always on show. As a result, it can become the focus of a great deal of stress and anguish for some lads when that all-important stubble fails to show.

Fast facts

● *Hair is completely natural. It grows on the body as a means of protection and insulation.*

● *There is no medical or hygienic reason to remove body hair.*

● *No link exists between bald men and virility. It's a myth!*

● *The male hormone, testosterone, is responsible for the growth of body hair.*

Body and facial hair may be a visible sign of maturity, but it isn't responsible for making you behave like a man. It's how you shape up on the inside that counts.

BODY ODOUR

On average, our bodies contain approximately 2.5 million sweat glands – tiny built-in air conditioners scattered under the surface of the skin. During puberty, the hormones rushing through your system tend to stimulate these glands, and the results can be a bit sweaty.

"My sister says my room smells like old socks, but I can't help it!"
Howard, 14

Body odour, or B.O. for short, is caused by bacteria found in sweat that's gone stale. It's particularly noticeable under the armpits and around the groin and nipples where the sweat glands are most concentrated. Everyone worries about whether they smell, girls as well as guys. In some

11

ways it's our body's way of keeping us on our toes about cleanliness. But there's no need to go dousing yourself in aftershave to mask a niff which may not even exist. There are plenty of things you can do to banish all whiff-worries.

‥iff know-how

Wash regularly with an anti-bacterial soap. This helps remove stale sweat and keep bacteria in order.

Concentrate particularly on washing under the armpits, where up to 80% of the body's sweat glands can be found.

Wear fresh underclothes every day, preferably cotton which lets the skin breathe.

Watch what you're eating. Spicy meals or foods such as onions or garlic can influence the way sweat smells

There are two types of product you can use to handle perspiration and body odour: anti-perspirant and deodorant. Before you buy, it's important to be aware of the difference between the two.

Anti-perspirants cut down on the amount you sweat, using a compound called aluminium chloride, while deodorants kill off the bacteria that cause sweat and smells.

A few people suffer from excessive sweating, where the body perspires more than necessary. If you're concerned contact your GP, because in some cases it could be a treatable medical condition.

Sort my spots!

"Spots have made my life a misery! I've had acne badly on my face and neck for the last two years and it's left me feeling so self-conscious that I rarely go out. Help!"
Dave, 16

Unzipped advice:

The best thing you can do is talk to your doctor about an effective acne treatment. If there's no change in eight weeks, ask to have the prescription changed.

At the same time, regain your confidence by understanding that looks really are skin deep. Even if your spots are the first thing people notice, it's your personality that shines through – and that can only happen if you learn to relax about your looks.

If spots aren't an issue for you, they won't be an issue for anyone else, and ultimately you will find treatment that works. So don't despair, just seek out the help you deserve!

Help, I stink!

I seem to be sweating a lot lately, and it's made me paranoid that I smell. What if girls pick up on it when I'm talking to them? It would be a disaster!
Wes, 14

Unzipped advice:

During puberty, hormones switch on sweat glands in your developing body, and hot flushes are often part of the package.

Things will soon settle down, but you don't have to let it rule your life. The key is to wash regularly, and wear fresh clothes against the skin every day – preferably cotton to let the skin breath.

For super-confidence, apply a deodorant or anti-perspirant to your pits after washing. Just avoid the temptation to drench yourself in aftershave. The packaging might promise it'll drive girls wild with passion, but too much is likely to drive them away. :o)

THE PERFECT SHAVE

When lads start shaving, it's often a bit of a hit and miss affair, resulting in raw skin, pimples and sometimes bloodshed! An electric shaver may be faster and less messy, but can be harsh on sensitive skin. So, if you want to go manual, and shave like a pro, here's how to leave yourself with skin like a baby's bum:

- **Buy yourself some razors.** *Your chemist will be stocked with a wide range – some with swivel heads that follow the contours of your face, while many feature two or even three blades so no whisker can escape.*

- **Wash your face.** *Use warm water to open pores.*

- **Apply shaving cream.** *Squirt a blob into your hand, and then use your fingertips to rub it over your face in circular motions.*

- **Fill a bowl with warm water.** *Not too hot, or you risk buckling the blade.*

- **Shave downwards.** *Use light strokes with the razor, rinsing each time. Avoid shaving against the grain of the hair, as this is what causes redness and irritation, which means following the direction in which the hair grows.*

- **Start at the sides.** *Followed by the moustache area, and finally the chin. This is because chin hairs are the toughest and need the most time to soften under the lather.*

- **Rinse off.** *With warm water, and pat your face dry.*

- **Avoid after-shave.** *As it contains alcohol which dries the skin. Instead, go for cold water to help close up pores, followed by a balm or moisturiser.*

3. private parts

"There are so many myths about willies that sometimes I can't tell what's true or false."
Robin, 14

"My dick bends to one side, am I abnormal?"
Jake, 13

"Why don't our bollocks live inside our bodies? At least we wouldn't have to worry about getting them caught in zips and stuff!"
Asif, 14

Your gags

Q: What is the name of the insensitive bit at the base of the penis?
A: The man!
Sol, 14

If puberty hasn't kicked in yet then brace yourself, because the contents of your boxers (your penis and your testicles) are going to attempt to become the centre of your world!

It's all down to the testosterone set to go surging through your system. Not only is this male hormone responsible for some important physical developments down there, it also switches you on sexually – so it's important that you know how to handle things …

THE TESTICLES

(testes, balls, bollocks, gonads, nads, cods, knackers)

You've got two of them. Each one is about the size of a walnut, shaped like rugby balls, and housed together in that sack (or scrotum) hanging just behind your willy. You might hear stuff about your balls 'dropping', (and it's true that as they mature during puberty your testes do descend from your groin into the sack), but it happens at a very slow rate – and really isn't anything to brag about.

"When my brother boasted about his balls dropping, I had visions of them bouncing off the floor and stuff! Then I went through puberty, and barely noticed it happening. Sure, you get hairier, and your balls get baggier and turn slightly darker, but that's it!"
Tom, 17

Ball points

● *Your balls aren't there for decoration. They serve an important purpose, and that's to produce sperm (minute tadpole-type things that join with a woman's egg, during sex, to make a baby).*

- Sperm is present in semen. This is the creamy, white-ish substance that shoots from your dick at the peak of sex or masturbation. It's basically sperm mixed with other fluids, and is sometimes called 'spunk' or 'come'.

- Sperm are very sensitive about temperature, and thrive slightly below body temperature. That's why your scrotum dangles out of the way, and shrivels up close to your body if it gets a bit nippy.

- Semen and pee pass down the same tube through the penis (but both can't happen at the same time). This tube is called the urethra.

- One ball, usually the left, hangs slightly lower than the other. This is believed to be nature's way of stopping them from smacking together when you run and making your eyes water.

- Small white dots may appear on the scrotum. This is where pubic hair will grow. They're harmless, and may also crop up at the base of the dick shaft.

- Unlike your brain, which is housed inside a tough skull, your nads need a little protection – so wear a box for games like football, hockey, rugby or cricket, and avoid idiots who think it's funny to flick you in the cods just to see how you react.

"There's nothing worse than catching a knock to the bollocks. For a split-second, you think it hasn't hurt, then this sick feeling rises and before you know it you're doubled up with tears in your eyes."
Zach, 15

THE PENIS
(knob, dick, cock, willy, todger)

As a child, your knob is no big deal, right? Grown ups don't have a problem if you toddle into the room with your winkle on full display, stand there clutching it for comfort, or let it spray all over the place when you take a leak and forget to hold on – even in public! It's just another bit of your body, like your foot or your ear. But then you grow up, become more sexually aware, and all of sudden that thing tucked away inside your trousers becomes a source of mystery and confusion, comparison and myth, insecurity and, sadly, sometimes shame.

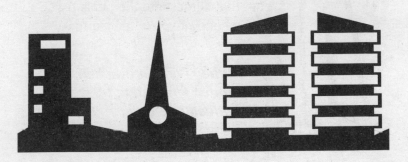

"I hated changing for games when I didn't have much pubic hair. I was terrified that my mates would start pointing and make me feel even more like the odd one out."
Brian, 13

Some lads might develop at a faster rate than others during puberty, but eventually we all end up with a pants package that serves the same function. There is no industry standard – no matter what your mates might say. What counts is that you're happy with what you've got, and understand that it's the content of your bonce that makes you a man, not the content of your boxers.

Erection section

When you're turned on sexually, the penis stiffens up. It grows longer, wider, and sticks outwards and upwards. This is called an erection. People sometimes call it a 'stiffy', a 'hard-on' or a 'boner' but there's no bone inside – just a lot of blood that surges into the penis tissue whenever you're feeling frisky.

"When I get an erection, it's almost impossible to concentrate on anything else!"
Danny, 15

It wasn't always this way. Erections can kick in from a very early age, but when you're a kid it's pretty much a random event that makes you feel a bit funny. It's only when you grow up, and become more switched on to your feelings, that the stirring between your legs become something loaded with sexual significance.

"I went through a stage of worrying that everyone could see I had an erection in my trousers."
Mick, 14

From puberty onwards, when erections crop up they're impossible to ignore. You don't even have to be thinking sexy thoughts to stoke up a trouser-arouser, so don't fret that you must be some kind of bus freak because it happens whenever you travel on one (it's a common occurrence – something to do with the throb and vibration of the engine!). It's also perfectly natural to conjure up an erection on demand – by rubbing your penis with your hand (see pages 36–38). Whatever it is that 'gives you wood', and whether it's a rare occurrence or a full time occupation, the trick is to relax about the whole issue – and focus on making sense of the emotions and sensations that go with it.

"There was a time when I thought my knob was totally out of control. I only had to think about someone I liked and it would spring up as if it had a mind of its own!"
Geordie, 16

Bendy stiffies: Some lads find their erections tend to curve towards the body, a bit like a banana. This is perfectly natural, just as it is to have a willy that hangs to one side when floppy. A bendy boner isn't the result of some hideous childhood accident, masturbating too much or sitting for too long with your legs crossed, and nor will it feel any different to a girl during sex. It's just the way you're made, and providing you don't make a big song and dance about it then nobody else will either.

Morning stiffies: A lot of boys get strung out about waking up with a hard on (sometimes called a 'morning glory'), but it's actually a common occurrence, and perfectly natural too. In fact, you might get an erection up to six times a night, but only know about the one you wake up with! It doesn't automatically mean you've been dreaming about sex, and if you choose to leave it alone it'll quickly fade away.

Ejaculation

So you're switched onto what your knob can do. It can grow hard, all on its own or with a helping hand through masturbation, but, like all the changes put in place by puberty, there is a purpose to having an erection – and it's called ejaculation.

At the point of peak sexual arousal, the muscles at the base of the penis contract. This causes semen (sometimes called 'come' or 'spunk') to spurt from the tip.
It only amounts to about a teaspoon in volume, and can be

thick and milky-white or clear and runny. On average, one load contains about 50 million sperm. Sometimes it can pump out like a pop from a water pistol, other times it's just a dribble. Either way, it's generally accompanied by what's called an 'orgasm' – as the muscles in your genitals prepare to make a delivery, so your heart rate rockets, your breathing quickens and an intense, pleasurable sensation washes through your body. It doesn't last long, in fact the buzz all but vanishes just after you've come.

"Coming for the first time was a shock, but a nice one."
Doug, 14

Fast facts

- *During an orgasm, contractions lasting about 3-15 seconds occur. Generally, the first three are most intense.*

- *It's not compulsory to have an orgasm when you ejaculate.*

- *You don't 'lose energy' by ejaculating.*

- *You can't run out of sperm (your testicles produce approx 200 million sperm every day, so no worries there).*

UNZIPPED INFORMER

Q: What are wet dreams?
Nicholas, 13

A: A wet dream is what happens when you ejaculate semen, or 'come', while sleeping. It's a perfectly natural and common occurrence during puberty. In some ways, it's your body's chance to carry out some test fire practice – just to check that everything is functioning properly. You may not even be aware of it happening, and simply wake to find a wet, sticky or dried patch of semen on the sheets. It can kick in a lot, or barely at all, but there's nothing to read into it – even the dreams responsible can be utterly random, and you may not recall them anyway. Sure, it might be a bit alarming the first few times, but whoever does the washing will have seen it all before, so there's no need to be ashamed – or feel compelled to take over laundry duties!

Size matters?

You might hear people talk about average penis size, but measuring up causes more problems than it's worth. The fact is, all dicks are different, and vary in both size and width depending on your state of arousal – not to mention temperature or how full your bladder is. Size really does bear no reflection on your status as a man and yet it still remains a number one worry. Some lads get into such a state, they even convince themselves that girls will reject them if it turns out they're packing teeny tiddlers.

"I used to fret that she'd take one look at my willy and laugh."
Gary, 15

"I'd heard that her ex was hung like a donkey, which made me feel really inferior."
Bo, 16

Now, blaming girls for all this penis anxiety is a bit unfair – especially because most women claim that size is not an issue when it comes to a man's sexual performance. Your old fella is basically designed to be in proportion with your body, and no lotion, potion, cream or pill is going to change that. Buying into the myth that dick size dictates whether you can stand proud or hide away from the world in shame does no lad any favours, gay or straight.

"Guys who brag about having big knobs are a big turn off, basically."
Jenny, 15

"I love my boyfriend because of who he is, not what he's got between his legs!"
Chris, 16

UNZIPPED INFORMER

Q: What's Jock itch?
Alfie, 14

A: A red and scaly rash on the upper thighs, caused by the same fungi responsible for Athlete's Foot. It's generally picked up by sharing towels with an infected person. Anti-fungal medication from your chemist or doctor will sort it out, but the problem can recur if you don't finish the treatment.

4. tackle it!

"I know how to look for breast cancer, because there's always features about it in my sister's magazines, but I've no idea how to check myself for testicle cancer."
Daniel, 16

"It's weird how lads obsess about their willies, but won't go to the doctor when they're worried something's wrong!"
Yasmin, 15

"I used to think I was addicted to masturbation, but then I realised a lot of lads my age can't leave it alone either!"
Lee, 14

It's one thing owning a penis and a pair of balls, but the only way you're all going to get along together is by knowing how to handle things – not just health-wise, but sexually too. It doesn't take much to check that everything is functioning properly, but it could save you a great deal of long-term grief.

THE FORESKIN

The penis is made up of two parts: the shaft, and the head (glans or helmet). The head of the penis is very sensitive, particularly around the rim. On the underside, you'll find the frenulum – a sensitive v-shaped band of skin that joins the head to the shaft. The penis head itself is covered by a loose, baggy sleeve of skin called the foreskin (unless you've been circumcised – see below). You should be able to roll the foreskin back to reveal the penis head and do an impression of a bald guy in a turtleneck, or see it emerge on its own accord when you get an erection.

UNZIPPED INFORMER

Q: What is circumcision?
Paul, 14

A: A simple operation to remove the foreskin from the penis. It's reckoned that 50% of all men in the world are circumcised, mostly for religious reasons (for example, in Muslim and Jewish faiths, all boys are circumcised in childhood). In rare cases, circumcision may be necessary on health grounds because the foreskin is too tight or baggy, but if it rolls back easily and you keep it clean there's no medical reason to have it removed. It won't make any difference to your sexual performance or virility.

UNZIPPED DIY: Foreskin health

Get inside the foreskin, and learn how to deal with some common problems.

SMELLY: The penis glands secrete a naturally occurring white or waxy deposit, which readily becomes occupied by a bug called smegma bacillus. It's perfectly natural, but, if left unwashed, the bacteria begin to break it down – and that can leave it smelling like Satan's socks.

Deal with it: Wash twice a day by gently retracting the foreskin and cleaning with unperfumed soap and water. Also be sure to dry the head thoroughly afterwards.

ITCHY: A red, inflamed foreskin and a super-sensitive bell-end are both symptoms of a condition called thrush. This is a harmless yeast infection that's common among women, but which can be passed on through sex.

Deal with it: Thrush can be treated easily with anti-fungal creams available from the chemist, such as Canestan. See your doctor if the problem persists.

BAGGY: A condition called phimosis, in which the uncircumcised foreskin cannot be pulled back beyond the widest part of the helmet. This often occurs in cases of excessive foreskin, or if the skin has been torn and then contracted during healing.

Deal with it: Take extra care over keeping things clean. Alternatively, circumcision may be in order – see your doctor if you're worried.

STRANGLED: Also known as paraphimosis, a rare condition in which a super-tight foreskin is pulled back over the head of the penis and gets stuck. This can lead to a painful inflammation of the glans that needs to be sorted quickly.

Deal with it: You'll need medical treatment before the foreskin can slide freely once more. If it's too swollen, the skin may be slit to allow more room to manoeuvre.

TESTICLE CARE

Your balls are responsible for production of both sperm and the male hormone testosterone. That makes them worth their weight in gold to you. Chances are they won't give you any grief, but if something does go wrong, be sure you know how to handle it.

TORSION: A term used to describe what happens when one ball twists and cuts off its own blood supply. It can occur due to a knock or a kick, but also for no apparent reason and even during sleep. Symptoms include unbelievable pain, nausea and fainting.

Deal with it: An emergency operation may be necessary to save the testicle.

SPERMATOCELE: A cyst-like lump that can be felt on the epididymis (the ribbed structure that runs up the back of your nads).

Deal with it: Generally it's harmless and no treatment is required, but always get checked out just to be on the safe side.

EPIDIDYMITIS: Bollocks feel like they're about to burst into flames. This painful condition is often associated with urinary tract infections, or STIs such as gonorrhoea and chlamydia (see chapter 8). Other symptoms can include fever and penis discharge.

Deal with it: See your doctor for antibiotics.

VARICOCELE: Varicose veins. One in ten men are thought to be saddled with swollen veins on the surface of their testicles. It's caused by problems with the valve mechanism responsible for controlling blood flow. Affected blokes report having plums that 'feel like a bag of worms'.

Deal with it: Surgery may be necessary in rare cases if it causes pain or is linked to infertility problems.

HYDROCELE: Ball sack fills up with fluid, often due to infection.

Deal with it: Antibiotics or surgery. Alternatively, your doctor may take a needle to your knackers and drain off the fluid – which sounds a lot worse than it actually is.

CANCER: Testicle cancer is the fourth biggest killer of men aged 15-34. Early signs include a swelling, lump, or dull ache in the scrotal area. Stomach or backache can also be a symptom, which may be a sign that the cancer is spreading.

Deal with it: Removal of the affected testicle (a simple operation) and possible chemotherapy or radiotherapy. Treatment for testicular cancer should not affect your sex life, or ability to father children, and treatment is very effective if caught early. Even so, just 3% of men regularly check their plums. If you don't know how, putting the next section into practice could save your life:

UNZIPPED DIY: Testicle check

When: once a month
Place: after a bath/shower
Duration: five minutes max

● *Cup your cods in the palm of your hands, leaving your fingers and thumbs free to feel around. The warmth of your bath/shower will have relaxed your sack, making it easier for you to check out the contents.*

- Get familiar with the size and weight of your testicles by gently rolling each one between your thumb and forefinger.

- You should feel a soft tube at the top and back of each bollock. This is called the epididymis, where the sperm is stored and ripens

- What you're looking for are strange lumps, bumps or hardening of the nuts.

- Be aware that it's usual for one testicle to be slightly larger than the other, or to hang at different levels.

- Don't freak out if you do find anything unusual, as it could be a harmless cyst, but do get it checked out with a doctor. There's absolutely no need to be embarrassed or ashamed, and if testicle cancer is caught early it does have a high treatment success rate.

UNZIPPED INFORMER

Q: Do tight pants cause infertility?

A: No, but close-fitting undies do tend to heat up your cods, which can slow down sperm production until you climb out of them again.

Q: Is it normal for one testicle to feel bigger than the other?

A: That's fine. Generally, it's the left testicle that hangs slightly lower than the right. It's lumps, bumps or persistent aches that you need to get checked out by your doctor.

Q: I was kicked in the nuts and it really hurt. Have I done myself a major injury?

A: A knock to the knackers can often cause considerable pain, but it doesn't necessarily means the damage is that bad. It can cause some swelling, and even blood in the semen, but generally things get back to normal after a few days. If in doubt, however, or problems persist, then make an appointment to see your doctor.

Q: Why do my balls get smaller when I have an erection?

A: It's believed to be self-protection mechanism, to stop the testes from getting knocked about during sex.

Q: Why does everything shrink when I go swimming?

A: It's nature's cruel joke, designed to show us up in front of girls! Biologically speaking, however, it's down to the simple fact that our testicles are temperature-sensitive. In cool water they tend to hurry back inside the body where it's warm – which doesn't leave much left to look at on the outside. The key is to stop fretting about it, because if you don't pay any attention to what's just shrivelled up inside your trunks then nobody else will either.

Q: I've noticed a lump on one of my nuts. It doesn't hurt, so should I leave it alone?

A: Any swelling in the scrotum should be checked out by your doctor. It's probably harmless, but testicle cancer can kill, so it's better to be safe than sorry.

DOCTOR, DOCTOR ...

Doctors generally have a big problem with boys – and that's their reluctance to ask for help when they think something's wrong with their tackle or anything else. While girls tend to feel more comfortable taking any intimate health concerns to their doctors, lads are more likely to grit their teeth and suffer in silence. Whether it's an itch, a spot, rash or sore, or even if it's just info they're after – pride and a misplaced sense of shame stop boys from asking for help. Which is weird, because anyone would think we'd be demanding daily check ups given the amount of love and attention we direct towards our bits!

"I'd never dream of showing my willy to my doctor. She's female, and a friend of the family!"
Scott, 14

The thing about doctors is that they've seen it all before. A knob is a knob to them, no matter where it's been or what you've done to it. Ultimately, you can't 'shock a doc', but you can strike up a good relationship with one and always be treated in complete confidence about any medical issue. At the same time you're always entitled to ask to see another medical practitioner, and nobody will hound you for a reason.

"My local surgery is miles away, and I didn't really want to ask my mum to drive me there, so I went to my school nurse instead. She was great, and because I needed some treatment she helped me tell mum. Even she was fine, and said she was just relieved that I'd got myself checked out."
Liam, 15

The bottom line is this: your doctor is there to help, but it's down to you to ask.

MASTURBATION

There are countless terms used to describe masturbation – the act of stimulating the penis to orgasm. From 'wanking off' to 'flogging the dolphin', 'beating your meat' or even 'choking the chicken', lads talk it up like an Olympic sport, and yet it's one of those strange taboos because nobody actually admits to doing it in private. As a result, a lot of myths have sprung up around the issue, and boys do worry that regularly tickling the pickle is somehow damaging to body and soul.

"I heard you shouldn't crack one off the wrist within twenty-four hours of a football match, because it leaves you feeling weak." (It doesn't!)
Guy, 15

"My mates say they toss off every day, but I don't. Does that mean there's something wrong with me?"
(Not at all!)
Richard, 14

36

Everyone discovers masturbation in different ways. Some lads find that fiddling about down there gives them a bit of a buzz, and pretty much progress into wanking as a full-time hobby, while others simply hear about it from mates, and decide to see what all the fuss is about.

"I didn't realise that I had masturbated before until someone explained to me what it was!"
Mark, 14

"I can't remember when I first did it, but I doubt I'll ever stop."
Warren, 16

At a time when your hormones are beginning to leave you feeling sexually supercharged, some lads do feel fit to burst unless they regularly tug at their trouser truncheons, but there really are no medical reasons to do so. Turn the page to get the facts.

- *Masturbation is totally normal, and certainly not a freakish thing to do.*

- *People do it whether they're single or in a relationship, male or female, and regardless of their sexual experience.*

- *It won't make you blind, insane, or stop you fathering children later in life.*

- *You won't get hairy palms as a result, and nor will your dick get worn down – though it might get a bit sore if you're repeatedly thrashing it.*

- *It's just something people choose to do because they enjoy it, but it's not compulsory and nor is it a reflection of your sex drive if you choose not to do it at all.*

- *Lads usually masturbate by gently gripping the penis in their hand and then moving it up and down to stimulate themselves towards orgasm. Let your dick dictate what works and what doesn't!*

- *There is no set time limit on how long or often you should masturbate, although, like anything you do on a regular basis that affects your mood, it can be a bit habit-forming.*

Masturbation is just a way of releasing sexual tension, and 'getting to grips' with the way your body works on a sensual level. It can help you learn to recognise when you're about to ejaculate, and achieve a satisfying climax, but it's not like eating – you won't suffer if you choose to leave it alone.

5. get connected: family life

"Mum always tidies my bedroom, which means there are no secrets between us!"
Alexander, 13

"I wish I could've talked to my dad before I came out as gay, but he was never around."
Brian, 14

"Mum and dad are tearing each other apart, but I feel I have to be strong for my little brothers."
Takumi, 15

Your gags

Q: How do you know if a man is lying?
A: His lips are moving!
Martin, 15

It's standard to have a bit of a love/hate relationship with your family. Living under the same roof can be a laugh, a comfort, or the last thing you need, often one after the other. Some lads come from huge, close-knit families, and hate it. Others find themselves in single-parent situations, with little or no money, and have a blast. There are no rules, because we're all brought up in different ways, in different situations, and that gives every one of us a unique experience of family life.

"My sisters wind me up all the time, especially if I bring mates back to the house, but my girlfriend gets on well with them."
Andy, 15

"I hated my stepdad when he first moved in, but he's like my best mate nowadays."
Greig, 14

Like or loathe your family, the trick is to make the effort, so that everyone under the same roof gets along as best they can. What's more, learning to connect with your nearest and dearest is a good primer for handling other relationships – not just friendships but in your love life too.

PARENTAL PROBLEMS

When you're caught up in worries of your own, it's easy to forget that other people have problems too – and that includes your parents. The same goes for step-parents and other carers too, because whoever looks after you will have their ups and downs, just as you do. None of this is your responsibility, of course, but if there are difficulties in their lives it can often have an impact on you. Here's how to deal with some common flashpoints.

Pushy parents

It's only natural for your folks to want you to excel in anything you do, especially when it comes to school and sport, but your happiness should also be a priority. Too much pressure can eat into your confidence and leave you feeling very stressed out indeed.

"My dad kept on about the straight A grades he felt sure I would get. I know he meant well, but it freaked me out!"
Brendan, 16

Deal with it: If you feel your parents' expectations are excessively high then tell them. They won't think any less of you, especially if you make it clear that you have your own drive and ambition. If anything, they'll admire the fact that you have the courage to be so honest. As long as you do your best, and aim to fulfil your own goals, then consider it a source of pride in itself.

Overprotective parents

Sometimes parents find it hard to accept that you're growing up, which can be frustrating for you. At a time when you feel the need for more freedom, a curfew or a check-up text from your folks every five minutes can leave you feeling suffocated.

"I was the only one to be under a nine o'clock curfew, which was so humiliating as all my mates could stay out much later."
Trent, 15

Deal with it: Show you're mature enough to handle the situation by negotiating with them, and reaching a compromise. Throwing a strop, marching out, or threatening to pack your bags is only going to confirm their fears. So keep your cool, and talk your way into making more space for yourself.

Embarrassing parents

Everyone, at some time or other, will have been deeply embarrassed by something a parent has done or said. Then again, most parents will be able to name an incident involving you that caused their cheeks to warm up! Sure, it can sometimes seem a bit bogus when your dad starts talking like a homeboy just to be in with your mates, but you have to respect the fact that at least he's making the effort.

"I knew my mum was due to collect me from the party, but I didn't expect her to knock on the door! I dreaded going to school the following Monday!"
Damien, 15

Deal with it: Aim to accept your parents for the way they are, and focus on the funny side. If you can all laugh at your own efforts to bridge the generation gap, you're more likely to meet in the middle.

Fighting parents

While some parents never have a cross word for each other, it's equally common to find couples that rarely seem to have anything civil to say. It doesn't always means their relationship is on the rocks, however. Sometimes that's just the way people communicate! But if it's making you anxious or you're fed up with it all, you have a right to make your feelings known.

"I know when my mum and dad have had a row because they barely talk to each other the next day."
Franz, 14

Deal with it: Your parents may not even be aware of the effect their slanging matches are having on you. Putting them in the picture might just bring them to their senses. It may not stop them from fighting, but it will make them take stock of the fact that they're not just hurting each other. They're hurting you too.

Physically abusive parents

Nobody has the right to use violence on you, and that counts for family members too. It's a form of abuse that can cause physical injury, emotional scarring, and make an innocent victim feel afraid to speak up.

"For eighteen months before he moved out, my dad terrified me. He used to push me about and call me names whenever he was stressed or drunk, and it left me feeling worthless. I did badly at school during that time and was basically trouble, but it wasn't until I started talking to my sisters that I began to realise that in a lot of ways he was responsible for that."
Iain, 16

Deal with it: The most courageous thing you can do is tell someone what's going on. You have a right to be safe, and help is out there to provide you with that protection. The National Society for the Prevention of Cruelty to Children (NSPCC) runs a confidential helpline for young people concerned about all issues of safety. Call Freephone 0808 800 5000, and talk to a trained counsellor. They will listen, and give you the confidence, advice and support you need to get your house in order.

Parents who part

An average of two out of five marriages in the UK winds up in separation or divorce. It can happen for many different reasons, sometimes simple, often complex, but a separation always leads to new family patterns taking shape. It's a big upheaval for all involved, but ultimately the grief you go through is the only way for everyone to find happiness again.

"When mum and dad split it felt like the end of the world. Now I live with my mum, and see my dad at weekends. As a result, I get on with them both much better."
Corey, 14

Deal with it: No matter what has come between your parents, even if they no longer seem to agree on anything, there's one thing that will always unite them – and that's your welfare. The key is to keep talking, and share your feelings about the changing situation. Things will settle down, but you have speak up if you want things to work out for you.

Alcoholic parents

Alcoholism is often called 'the family disease' because it affects everyone surrounding the drinker. It's a destructive force, causing unpredictable and extreme behaviour, lying and even violence. What's more, a drinking problem can develop so slowly over time that you may not even click that a parent's behaviour is unusual. Living in this kind of environment isn't healthy. It can seriously damage your self-esteem, leave you feeling unloved, sensitive to conflict, and even shape the way you handle future relationships.

"Sometimes I feel like saying my dad's dead. It seems easier than explaining that he has a disease that means he's dependent on alcohol."
Sanun, 15

Deal with it: You are not to blame for someone's drinking habit, but neither can you force them to cut down or quit. All you can do is make them aware of the effect their habit has on you, and let them know you're prepared to help them overcome the problem. At the same time, take steps to look after yourself. If you feel unable to confide in another family member, call DrinkLine on 0800 917 8282 and talk in confidence to a trained counsellor. Also give the number to the parent in question. When they're ready to face up to the problem, they'll know where to turn for advice and support.

BONDING WITH BROTHERS AND SISTERS

We tend to have the same rollercoaster relationship with our siblings as we do with our parents. If you have any brothers or sisters, then chances are you can think of several occasions where you couldn't have done without them, and others where you wish they'd never been born! But then, it's important to remember that they probably feel the same way about you . . .

Feeling jealous

When you're jostling for attention from your folks, it's easy to get a bit uptight if it feels like someone else in the family is getting more than you. The trouble with sibling jealousy is that it rarely goes away on its own. Usually it builds up over time, until you can't take it any more and kick off with no warning. But it doesn't have to be this way.

"My mum kept showering praise on my brother because he got a good school report, but it only made sense when I found out he'd also been bullied that term."
Richard, 13

Deal with it: Being envious of your siblings is a sign that you could feel better about yourself. The fact is we're all good at different things, but parents will usually do their utmost to ensure that you all get the same level of praise and recognition. If you genuinely feel left out, however, then it's important to speak up. At the very least, it'll give your folks a chance to flag up your talents and help develop them.

Feeling cloned

So you know who you are, where you're at, and where you're going. It's taken a while to suss your identity and refine your image, and the future's looking bright. Then a younger brother (or even a sister) pitches up beside you and cramps your style by looking like a lite version of you.

"I felt like he'd stolen a piece of me."
Joey, 15

Deal with it: Instead of viewing their behaviour as wholesale theft of your image, turn the tables and view it as a compliment. Unlike you, they're just starting to work out what makes them tick, and they see you as a bit of a role model. You're cool in their eyes – the dude who walks and talks just like they feel they should! Instead of stropping about it, why not help them work on their identity? Give them some hints and tips, and they'll soon find the confidence to find their own place in the world.

5. get connected: your mates, your love life

"I didn't feel comfortable telling my mates that my dog had died in case I start crying in front of them."
Stuart, 13

"My friends are party hounds, but we're running out of invitations."
Bruce, 15

"When she asked what I was doing at the weekend I just didn't know what to say. I'd fancied her for ages, but never expected her to make all the moves!"
Marc, 14

WHAT ARE FRIENDS FOR?

Right now, your mates probably feel like the most important people in your life. You hang out together, share dodgy jokes and disses, even heated arguments about match performance or kung fu technique. It's important that you can count on your friends for a laugh.

But this can mean that a great deal goes unspoken – and that's all the fears and insecurities and questions whirling around your head about sex and girls and your mindset –

stuff you feel unable to open up about for fear of laughter and ridicule.

"My best mate and me do everything together, but when my parents were splitting up it just wasn't a subject for discussion. I had all this grief going on in my life but I didn't want to show it in case he misunderstood."
Dorian, 15

Communicating with mates about real issues is tough. We can talk about trivial fluff without hesitation, but when it comes to discussing personal stuff we tend to clam up or start bluffing. This is partly down to lack of practice, because boys aren't often encouraged to speak on intimate terms, but mostly down to a fear of being ridiculed. With so much bravado knocking around among lads, about anything from snogging to dick size, it's very hard to get serious about things like health or relationship issues.

"All my friends claim they're well hung, so all I can do is say I have a big one too!"
Marcus, 13

Chances are your friends are all in the same boat. Like you, they probably spend more time covering up for their own insecurities and doubts than by seeking advice they can trust. When everyone says they're 'fine, no worries', for example, you're unlikely to chip in that you cried yourself to sleep the night before. As a result, we bundle through our teen years buying into more myths and succumbing to peer pressure in case we stand out from the crowd and invite more grief.

This reluctance to open up about what's really going on inside our heads can exist long after our adolescence, and affect the way we handle future relationships. Which is a shame, because lads who do brave talking to a friend they trust on a more emotional level find themselves rewarded in many ways. When it comes to forging lasting friendships, it's possibly the most courageous thing you can do. Check out the benefits:

● *The chance to express yourself. Opening up can only help get problems in perspective.*

● *A release valve. Getting something off your chest feels so much better than brooding about it.*

● *An opportunity to relate to another experience. You're not alone, after all.*

"I don't have to brag to my best mate, or pretend I've done things he hasn't so I feel big. Being honest about what I don't know is more of a laugh than making up stories and hoping nobody questions me, plus I get a chance to check my facts about things I've heard."
Garth, 14

DEALING WITH GIRLS

Lads have a strange relationship with girls their own age. As kids, we appear to get on well enough, apart from the dresses and the thing they have about dolls. Then we start to go our separate ways, encouraged by differing interests, pursuits and outlooks on life. By the time we're into double figures we might as well be on different planets, which is a pain, really, because that's when we start to get interested in each other again.

"I know I fancy a girl if I find myself thinking about her a lot."
Tony, 13

"I had no idea how to talk to her, or what to say. Every time I tried to start a conversation I'd feel my heart race."
Marcus, 13

Puberty is largely responsible for encouraging this about-turn in attitude towards the opposite sex. As hormones beef up your body for adulthood, so it deepens your emotional needs, and that can encourage many boys to become more involved with girls. The trouble is, after so many years of avoiding them, our social skills can be a little lacking.

"She's out of my league. Simple as that. What would she see in me?"
Will, 15

Relationship round up

Connecting with girls as friends is not so different from hooking up with other lads on your wavelength. Quite simply, your shared interests or outlooks make it happen. It's when you find yourself drawn to a girl on a physical and emotional level that all manner of doubts and insecurities kick in, none of which are eased by the pressure you can feel from your peers.

"Every time she came into the classroom, my mates would make life hell for me. They'd whistle and jeer, basically because they knew I fancied her."
Ed, 14

There is no magic solution formula for developing a relationship with a girl. A great deal is down to experience, the confidence to rise above that standard-issue ribbing from your mates, and then following Unzipped's three Bs:

- *Be yourself*
- *Be relaxed*
- *Be respectful*

Just don't go thinking that going out with a girl will make you a happier, more complete individual. If you're only hoping to date because you think it'll impress other people, then it won't be very rewarding for either of you. In fact, you don't have to date anyone at all. It's not compulsory, and you'll learn more about yourself as a free agent than by rushing into a relationship for the wrong reasons. Ultimately, when it comes to advice you can trust on this matter, why not ask the girls!

Inside girls' minds

Cut out some of your grief and anxiety, right here.

"I like lads who are fun to be with, and who treat me as a friend."
Karen, 14

"Guys are sweet when they understand that we can be just as nervous as them."
Bee, 16

"A boy doesn't have to be romantic to win me over, or fall head over heels in love. He just has to be interested in me as a person. If we click, that's great!"
Sal, 15

"Any lad who can look me in the eyes, instead of staring at my chest!"
Pippa, 17

"Boys who make me laugh, as long as they don't try too hard."
Harriet, 15

… and what they don't want:

"Boys who get their mates to ask a girl out."
Stephanie, 16

"Any lad who blows hot and cold. It just shows they're not mature enough to handle their feelings."
Danielle, 15

"Guys who spend more time playing video games than talking to me!"
Victoria, 14

"I hate to feel like a trophy girlfriend. It's the worst kind of turn-off."
Andrea, 15

"I went on a date with a lad who turned up with his mates. It was the last time we went out together!"
May, 15

How do I ask her out?

This is perhaps the most common question to any problem page, and one with a simple answer: you don't! Let's face it, the prospect of asking someone directly for a date is enough to bring on a sleepless night beforehand. What's more, after all the fear and insecurity you're bound to go through in working up the courage, your question can only invite a 'yes' or a 'no' response. Now, chances are she's going to be shocked if you steam in and ask her out, and it may result in a knock-back, even if she shares your feelings. Here's how to make that move without breaking a sweat or winding up with a red face.

● *Steer clear of chat up lines. Girls don't think they're big or clever, especially those intended to make them feel stupid so you look smart (or so you hope).*

● *Treat her like a friend, not a girlfriend in waiting. Get to know her better, and see what makes her tick. There's no need to be profound or impressive. You don't need a comedy routine up your sleeve to win her over. Just be yourself.*

● *Spend time together. The more you hang out, the more relaxed you'll be in her company, which can only help the real you shine through. It'll also give you a chance to suss out how she really feels. If there's a spark, you'll soon know. And if a date doesn't happen by default . . .*

● *Be honest. If your friendship has grown, and you'd like to take things further, then let her know. Don't spring it as a big surprise, or expect an instant answer, but do keep an open mind when you talk about it. As for a date, there's no need to mention the word itself. Just keep it simple and suggest a trip to the cinema or something you both enjoy. Hopefully you'll get the response you've been waiting for – a date without even trying – but at the very least you'll have made a good friend.*

What if I fall in love?

A relationship can mean as much or as little as you like. It helps if you both feel the same way about each other, and that you're relaxed enough to open up about what's going on inside your head and heart. Even then, you don't have to be in love to have a good time together, or feel somehow that you have to make it last for ever. Many relationships work out just fine based on mutual affection and respect. They may not last for ever, but if it was fun for you both while it lasted then it would've been worthwhile.

Love is a word that's often knocked about like a football, but don't shoot to score unless you really mean it. We're talking about a powerful emotion, after all, and one that often builds over time. It can be a buzz when it does kick in, but it isn't compulsory and nor does it make you more complete than someone who is single. So what is love and how do we handle it?

Love is many things, but ultimately, if you feel a deep sense of admiration, respect, attraction, trust and passion then you'll find a natural time and place to sum it up in three words: 'I love you.'

- *Don't feel pressured into saying it, or be fooled into thinking it's a shortcut to sex. Nor is it a guaranteed way of making someone stay in a relationship. It's just something you choose to say that can deepen the bond between you, providing it comes from the heart.*

- *Being in love can often go without saying, even in some of the most rewarding relationships. If you're constantly holding out to hear it from your other half, it could be a sign of insecurity on your part. Don't brood, however, but discuss what's going on together. In some ways, sharing this kind of intimacy is where true love lies.*

Review your feelings. Being in love with someone is a blast, but it doesn't mean you'll be an item for ever. Sometimes love can make things too intense, it can just burn out, or one of you may not feel able to return the same feeling. It's no cause for shame or embarrassment, but as one half of the relationship you have a responsibility to deal with it sensibly.

When it's over

Breaking up is never easy, whether you're the one who wants to split, or you find yourself being chucked. It forces you to deal with the downside of love, but it is an important part of learning about relationships. Handle it right, and you can only come away stronger for the experience.

If you've been dumped ...

Don't blame yourself. You're just the same lad this person fell for in the first place. What has changed are the other person's feelings and needs. You have to respect their honesty, and aim to come out of this relationship with positive memories.

Accept the situation. Being dumped can come as a shock, but try to avoid pinning your hopes on a second chance, or reacting badly when you learn it's over. It's great if you can both talk it over and make sense of what has happened. Just be aware that sometimes relationships end with no real explanation. This can be hard, but if you hang out for a reason that doesn't really exist, it's only going to eat you up. Whatever the circumstances behind the split, even if it's messy, here's how to move on.

Express yourself: Let's face it, getting the elbow can be a choker, and if you feel like crying then bring it on. OK, so you may not fancy blubbing in front of all your friends, but one good mate will understand, and confiding in him will help you through this difficult time.

Surround yourself with friends and family: Turn to people you trust, and let them remind you that being a free agent can be fun. You will hurt for a while, because you've lost someone you care about, but in time you will accept it's over – and the experience can only set you up to handle future relationships.

If you're finishing things ...

Be truthful. It's better to be honest, knowing that it's going to hurt, than to continue going out together even though your heart isn't in it. Think how you'd feel if the tables were turned, and this person was only keeping the relationship going out of pity!

Avoid compromise. It's tempting to stress that you'd like to stay close friends because it seems like a good way to soften the blow. The trouble is you risk creating false hope for your soon-to-be-ex, which can only make things harder for you both. So make a clean break, and give yourself both time before deciding if you'd like to see each other again.

Don't run away from the situation, and ignore them or get off with someone else. Sure, it sends out the signal that you're not interested any more, but it doesn't show much respect or maturity.

UNZIPPED INFORMER
Love is the drug!

Strip away the romance and the roses, and you'll find that love is triggered by a chemical change in the brain.

Phenylethylamine is the name of the naturally-occurring substance that kicks in when you fall for someone you fancy. It's responsible for an increased heart rate, sweating palms and blissful feelings. High levels of the 'love drug' can also be found in chocolate!

She talks too much!

"My girlfriend keeps telling everyone all about us! As a result, I have to put up with stupid jokes from her mates. I've tried talking to her about this, but she laughs and says I'm being silly."
Shane, 14

Unzipped advice:

No one likes their undies aired for all to see, and your girlfriend needs to know there are some things you'd rather keep under wraps. Basically, she needs to spend more time listening to you than talking about you. But, before you raise the subject again, be aware that this is one subject where there's a real male/female divide.

While the lads are probably only interested in knowing if you did one thing, girls love to analyse whole relationships. Your girlfriend wants to be seen to be having fun in her romance with you. At the same time, she's keen to check this relationship is functioning normally. By talking to her friends, she can find this out for herself. Meanwhile, you mustn't bottle up your own feelings on the subject. It you keep quiet, you'll only end up resenting her for talking so much. That's why you need to get together and lay down some ground rules.

Maybe there are some things which you're happy for her to share with her friends, but she should know if there's any stuff which is special to you because it's private. She'll probably really appreciate you opening up to her in this way. While it should help her to understand your feelings, just don't forget to respect hers.

7. switching on to sex

"On my fourteenth birthday, my dad sat down with me and said I could ask him anything I liked about sex. I was horrified! We'd never mentioned the word before, and I couldn't wait to get out of the house!"
Stephen, 15

"I'm always having dreams about sex. The trouble is I can never remember the details!"
Russ, 14

"I knew that I was gay from an early age, but I didn't tell anyone until I felt absolutely confident about what that meant to me. It took years, but I'm glad that I didn't rush into coming out."
Pete, 18

Your gags

Q: How can you tell if a man is feeling horny?
A: He's breathing.
Lal, 15

Sex plays such a central role in our society that we become aware of it from an early age. It's all over the telly, from adverts to soap operas, on billboards and in films and magazines – not necessarily explicit stuff, but images and storylines that slowly reinforce the idea that sex is somehow a very big deal indeed. Of course, as kids, it's just something to giggle and snarf about, but when puberty hits and other lads start bragging about their conquests, it's easy to think you're out of the loop and somehow less of a man.

"My mates talk about sex all the time, and everyone seems to have something to say about it. The trouble is nobody questions anything, and that makes it impossible to know what to believe."
Sid, 14

"The day my best mate announced he'd lost his virginity, I suddenly felt like he'd left me behind."
Harry, 16

For many boys, the pressure to appear like natural born shag champs with nothing more to learn means that sex becomes an issue for very wrong reasons. It breeds anxiety, a lot of covering up for stuff we don't understand, and the creation of some dangerous myths. The endless bragging and pilfered porn mags that do the rounds can also lead lads to believe that sex for its own sake is what it's all about, rather than linking it to relationships and emotions. In fact, your mates are possibly the biggest source of misinformation there is. So if you want to be

sussed then find an alternative source of info you can trust
– one that allows you to seek answers to your questions
without feeling embarrassed or afraid.

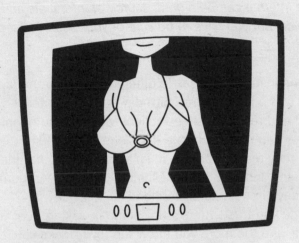

- *Parents are often a good source of info, because you can ask stuff when your mates aren't around. Sadly, many mums and dads aren't always available, or feel unable or unwilling to help because sex isn't something you've talked about in the house before. If you can overcome the initial embarrassment, however, and find the time and place to talk, you'll find the subject becomes easier to discuss.*

- *Older family members like brothers or sisters can sometimes seem easier to approach about the subject of sex, often because you're on the same wavelength.*

- *Your school library or sex-education class is another good place to get nitty-gritty facts.*

- *Your doctor, local NHS sexual health (GUM) clinic or Brook Advisory Centre (0800 0185 023) will be happy to chat privately about any worries you have.*

- *The Internet can be a great source of info, facts and advice, but you have to be sure of your sources (see contacts).*

Everyone learns about sex in different ways, but no lad wakes up on his sixteenth birthday feeling suddenly primed and ready for sheet-action! Many young people feel they can make sensible decisions about their lives before they reach that age, in spite of the fact that the law makes sex under 16 illegal. Ultimately, if you're in doubt about any sex-related issue then check it out with someone you trust! There's no shame in asking questions, after all, and the more you know the fewer risks you're likely to take.

SEXUAL FANTASIES

It's natural to think about sex, no matter what your experience. Whether you're the world's greatest studmuffin, or still waiting for that first kiss, your mind's eye will gladly screen X-rated thoughts whenever it takes your fancy. It's just one way for you to get in touch with your sexuality, impulses and desires. Even so, a lot of lads stress out about the kind of adult-only imagery that drifts into their heads.

"I keep thinking about what it would be like to have sex with my French teacher, which makes it hard for me to look her in the eye!"
Ewan, 15

"I found myself wondering what it would be like to kiss a boy, and that freaked me out."
Saul, 14

Fantasy facts

- *A fantasy is an escape from reality.*

- *Think of it as your head testing out some scenarios to help you master the feelings they stir up. These aren't necessarily a reflection of your real life needs, however, and that can include fantasies about other lads.*

- *Fancying celebrities, teachers, or even other people's parents is another form of fantasy, and a safe first step towards handling more realistic relationships.*

- *A fantasy can mean as much or as little as you want, but it only becomes an issue if you make it one. As long as*

67

you're honest with yourself, you don't have to explain it to anybody.

- *If you do feel the need to open up to make sense of what's going on in your head, make sure you do so to someone you trust.*

SEXUALITY

Everyone becomes aware of their growing sexual feelings in different ways, and it can be confusing to find you're attracted to other boys. Being gay or homosexual (attracted to members of the same sex) or bisexual (attracted to both sexes) can have a big influence on your life or very little. Some people know what makes them tick from an early age, while many others aren't so certain, or get mixed up about admiring other lads and fancying them. What's important is that you feel able to talk about your sexuality, and learn to incorporate it into your life so that you're happy, confident, and tolerant of others.

Coming out

"I told a friend that I was gay. The next day, the whole school knew. Looking back, the hassle I got as a result was minor compared to the fact that a friend had betrayed my confidence."
David, 16

Your sexual identity is a personal thing. Nobody can tell you whether you should fancy boys, girls, or both, or even change your mind at any time! That's your decision. At the same time, if you know you're gay, only you can decide if and when the time is right to tell people. It's especially difficult if you're young and male, because going public about your sexuality can invite untold grief and misery from other lads. There are many reasons why anti-gay (or homophobic) feeling runs rife through macho culture, but it's largely based on fear, stupidity and ignorance. The only way to stamp out this kind of prejudice is by encouraging people to review their beliefs. How? By leading your life with openness, honesty and respect for others.

"A lot of boys I knew treated me like a freak when I said I was bisexual, and it was tough to deal with. I focused on the fact that my real mates accepted me for who I am, and slowly people realised that giving me a hard time basically reflected badly on them."
Lee, 15

You have every right to go public about your sexuality. You may feel it's better to be open and honest than to feel like you're living with a secret, but you do have to be prepared to handle the impact it will have on your life. Here are some of the things to think about first.

- **Don't rush:** *Everyone who comes out will have a different story to tell, but they'd all agree that you should be fairly confident about your sexuality first. Maybe you've known for ages, but if it's something you've only been thinking about for a short time then it won't hurt to wait a while. Think ahead – you don't want to tell everyone you're gay if there's a chance you'll have second thoughts at a later date. What's more, it's just a way of labelling yourself. It won't change who you are inside, so don't go thinking that coming out will make your feelings any easier to handle. That comes with understanding yourself.*

- **Turn to someone you trust:** *If you feel that coming out is the right thing to do, confide in someone who can give you the support and understanding you need to tell others. A family member, close friend, teacher or school counsellor are often a good starting point. If you would rather open up to someone outside the situation, call the Lesbian & Gay Switchboard (see contacts) and talk in confidence to trained counsellors. They can relate to your experience and help you think about what your feelings mean.*

- **Only you can find the right words:** *Just be aware that you don't have to justify your sexuality to anyone but yourself, and use the opportunity to talk through the way you feel. If anything, it'll help you get a clearer perspective on things.*

- **Be prepared:** *Sadly, some people won't react as you had hoped. They might be shocked, misinformed about homosexuality, or simply hold anti-gay views. Whatever* the case, all you can do is stress that essentially you're still the same person as you were before you came out. All that's different is their perception of you, and the fact is attitudes can be changed. You may find they just need some time to accept things. You can help them by just getting on with your life and showing that being gay is just one more aspect of who you are.

VIRGIN STATES

"I couldn't wait to pop my cherry, and ended up losing it to a girl I barely knew. It was all a bit shabby really. I don't regret it, but things could've been better."
Todd, 16

"I haven't had sex yet, but that doesn't make me any different from my mates."
Perry, 15

Virginity has a bit of an image problem. It's one of those things that many lads regard as something to get rid of and fast! Thanks to peer pressure, it becomes a source of shame and humiliation – something stopping you from being a full-on adult. It's only when you start asking what you're actually losing that you realise what a load of rubbish this is. Being a virgin bears no reflection on your personality, and yet still boys rush into sex and wind up feeling let down, disillusioned, embarrassed or worse.

"I didn't use a condom the first time I had sex because I was too nervous to ask if she had one. I was terrified I'd got her pregnant as a result, or even caught a disease. I'd never take such a stupid risk again."
Keith, 17

"Sex can be over hyped by boys. My first time was over really quickly, but it was nice just lying with my girlfriend afterwards. I think if I'd lost my virginity to someone I didn't care for, it would've been horrendous!"
Aaron, 18

THINKING ABOUT SEX

Let's say you've met someone special, and sex is on the cards. Before you steam ahead, just take a moment to ask if you're truly ready, or if it's even right for your relationship. You might have turned into a couple of snog-monsters, but that doesn't mean things have to get any more physical if you're both happy as you are. If you're in any doubt as to whether sex is going to be a safe and rewarding experience then be smart and put your passions on hold. There's no hurry, after all, and you can use the time to address any doubts or worries you might have. Finding out the facts together can even help you feel more relaxed with each other, but it doesn't follow that you have to put your research into practice! The closer you are on an emotional level, the easier it is to deal with the physical side of things without feeling pressured or rushed.

Sex for the wrong reasons:

- *Everyone else says they've done it.*
- *You feel ashamed to be a virgin.*
- *You think it'll earn respect from your friends.*
- *You feel it'll make you more of a man.*
- *You're worried about saying no.*
- *You don't want to lose your girlfriend.*

THE SCORE WITH THE LAW

1 According to the Sexual Offences Act 2003, it is illegal for any kind of sexual activity to take place between two people if one or both participants is under 16.

2 The law applies to men and women, whatever their sexuality, in England and Wales. The same law applies in Northern Ireland, except the age of consent is 17.

3 The law exists to protect young people from abuse by adults. It isn't intended to outlaw consensual teenage sexual behaviour.

8. sex essentials

"Lads should carry condoms and not worry what people think. From a girl's point of view, it shows respect. End of story."
Tanya, 17

"Sex for its own sake is a bit rubbish, frankly. It's just so much more rewarding when it's with someone you love."
Andrea, 18

"The more I understand about sex, the easier it is for me to deal with all the jokes about being a virgin. It doesn't bother me, and if it bothers other people that's their problem."
Phil, 16

CONTRACEPTION

Even if you're not in a relationship at the moment, but you think there's a chance you might sleep with someone, it's vital that you take steps to protect yourself against unwanted pregnancy and sexual infections.

CONDOMS: Not just good for water balloons ...

● *A condom is a thin latex sheath that fits over an erect penis. Most are coated in a slippery water-based lubricant to help make sex more comfortable. When you ejaculate, the sperm is caught in a little teat at the top, which physically prevents it from entering the vagina.*

● *Condoms (rubbers, johnnies) are the only form of contraception that offers up to 98% effectiveness against the risk of pregnancy as well as sexual infections, including the HIV virus.*

● *There are many alternative contraception methods for women, such as the oral contraceptive pill, but don't just leave it up to her to take precautions – using a condom as well as another form of contraception can only make things extra safe.*

● *Taking an active in role in choosing the right contraception shows respect for yourself as well as your partner. If anything they'll be relieved and pleased that you made the effort.*

● *Condom practice makes perfect, especially if you're unsure how to use one, or just want to see how it feels! You'll find simple-to-follow instructions inside every packet.*

● *Condoms are widely available, over the counter from the chemist, in supermarkets, petrol stations, college vending machines and public toilets. You don't have to be 16 to buy or get condoms.*

- *Whatever brand you choose, ribbed, flavoured, whatever – check the 'use by' date and make sure it has the British Kitemark (EN600:1996) on the box, as well as the CE Mark. All it means is they meet a certain quality and you can trust them to get the job done!*

- *OK, so nobody really enjoys buying condoms in public, but the person behind the till will be entirely numb to your unease. They don't care. They've seen it all before. You might as well be buying toothpaste!*

- *Free condoms are available from some doctors, family planning clinics or your local Brook Advisory Centre (0800 0185 023). All these places are also a good source of friendly and confidential info and advice about contraception and sexual health.*

- *People won't think carrying condoms means you assume you'll be seeing some sheet action. It just means you're sussed about safer sex and prepared for all eventualities.*

THE MORNING-AFTER PILL

This is another name for the emergency contraceptive pill – for women only! To be effective, it has to be taken within 72 hours (three days) of unprotected sex or if the chosen method of contraception fails (i.e. if a condom splits). In practical terms, the sooner it is taken, the better. The morning-after pill can be obtained from a doctor or clinic, and from some chemists. Even so, it is not recommended for regular use.

STIs: THE UNZIPPED FILES

Sexually transmitted infections (STIs) can be passed from one person to another during sex. There are lots of different types of STI, including the HIV virus which can lead to AIDS. Often the symptoms aren't visible, and can damage your long-term health if left untreated.

Recent research suggests that less than one in three 16-24 year olds have heard of chlamydia, one of the most common STIs, compared to more than 90% who have heard of herpes and HIV.

The best way to avoid STIs is by using a condom every time you have sex. Unprotected sex (sex without a condom) greatly increases the risk of picking up or passing on an infection. This means it's worth using one, even if you're with a girl who's on the contraceptive pill, which provides no STI protection. Here's a breakdown of the main offenders, plus tips on spotting the symptoms.

Chlamydia

10% of sexually active UK teens are believed to have this common infection, with the majority of all female cases showing no apparent symptoms. If left untreated, it can leave you unable to have children later in life.

Symptoms: A stinging sensation when you pee, discharge from the penis, testicle pain.

Treat it: A simple course of antibiotics, available from your doctor or clinic.

Genital herpes

A virus called Herpes simplex (type II). It's sexually transmitted, and lasts for life.

Symptoms: Herpes can lie dormant for months, and then flare up in the form of burning genital blisters and sores. Flu-like symptoms usually accompany an outbreak. Steer clear of sex when herpes is active, even using condoms.

Treat it: Anti-viral drugs can minimise the frequency and intensity.

UNZIPPED INFORMER

Q: What's a GUM clinic?

A: GUM is medical shorthand for Genito-Urinary Medicine. It's basically a sexual health clinic and part of your NHS hospital (call your local hospital switchboard for details). It's open to anyone who wants help, advice and info on any sexual health matter, and that includes free testing and treatment for sexually transmitted infections. It's completely confidential, which means any visit or treatment won't become part of your general medical records. What's more, you can make your own appointment without going through your doctor.

Genital warts

A virus called HPV that is passed on by skin-to-skin contact, mostly during sex.

Symptoms: White or pinkish lumps on the skin around the

genital area. Mostly painless, sometimes itchy.

Treat it: Warts can be easily removed by your doctor or clinic. Never attempt to do this yourself.

Gonorrhoea

This infection has been a risk for thousands of years, but it's on the increase again.

Symptoms: Kicks in two to ten days after oral, anal or vaginal sex with an infected person, and include yellowish or creamy discharge from the penis, tenderness in the testicles and possible flu-like symptoms.

Treat it: Antibiotics will sort it out, but be sure to finish the course.

HIV

HIV is a virus that can lead to AIDS, an incurable illness that stops the body's immune system from functioning properly. HIV can live in the body for up to ten years without any symptoms, though it will continue to multiply and eventually mess with the body's ability to fight off infection. The virus is present in the blood, semen or vaginal fluid, which means it can be passed on through unprotected sex (vagina, anal and, in some cases, oral) and/or sharing needles for drug use.

Symptoms: If you think you're at risk, or believe you've been exposed to HIV, then get checked out immediately. Contact your doctor, local GUM clinic or Brook Advisory Centre (see Contacts).

Treat it: There is no cure for AIDS. Medical advances continue for people with HIV, but the incidence of infection is on the increase. Ultimately, a condom could save your life.

Pubic lice

Crab-like critters, no bigger than a pinhead, that live and breed in your pubes. They're caught from sex, infected bedding, clothes and towels.

Symptoms: Itching is the main effect, as the beggars are basically sucking your blood.

Treat it: A lotion from your doctor or GUM clinic will put an end to your pubic misery.

STI Primer

- *Unprotected penetrative sex isn't the only way that some STIs are passed from person to person.*

- *Some STIs can be transmitted through genital contact.*

- *Not all STIs produce noticeable symptoms.*

- STIs like herpes can be transmitted through oral sex (kissing, licking or sucking your partner's genitals, or having this done to you).

- Safer sex means being switched on about the risk of pregnancy, STIs, and the steps you can take to protect yourself and your partner. Always use a condom, and if you suspect you might have an infection then get checked out asap. It makes sense for the sake of your health, your future partners and your chances of fathering children later in life.

- If you do pick up an infection, be sure to tell any sexual partners who could be at risk or who might've transmitted it to you. There's no point being emotional about it, by dishing out blame or feeling guilty. The responsible thing to do is just deal with it, and reduce the risk of the infection spreading.

YOUR SEX QUESTIONS

All the stuff you'd never dream of asking your mates

Q: What's French kissing?

A: It's another word for snogging, which involves two people locking lips and letting their tongues play around with each other. It's not rocket science, nor is it to be confused with the kind of kiss you give your granny when she comes to visit. In the right place and with a partner you care about, it's just an intimate form of kissing that can be as mind-blowing as sex itself.

"There are no kissing rules, so long as you're slow, sensual and considerate, and don't just jam your tongue down the throat. Yuk."
Sasha, 16

Quick Quiz

Q: The clitoris is:

1. A 300-metre sprint event, in which competitors vault a serious of fences wearing clown wigs and comedy shoes.

2. A highly sensitive fleshy bump that lies just in front of the opening of the vagina. Gently stimulating your partner's clitoris will help arouse her and can often lead to female orgasm.

A: The answer is 2.

Q: What's foreplay?

A: Think of it as the warm up session before the match itself. You can't just steam onto the pitch and expect to perform perfectly, and in some ways it's the same in the sack. Foreplay is basically the name given to any form of touching, caressing, stroking, whispering or kissing that takes place before intercourse (although it doesn't always lead to penetration). This kind of intimate contact helps you relax and get comfortable, and gives you a chance to explore each other's bodies, while physically serving to arouse you both. For a girl, this means her vagina will become warm and moist in readiness for the penis to enter.

"There's nothing worse than a lad who thinks sex is all about penetration. Sometimes foreplay can be just as satisfying."
Sophie, 17

Q: "I don't know what a blow job is!"

A: A blow job is properly known as oral sex, and is often referred to as 'giving head' or 'going down'. It describes a sex act in which the man's penis is kissed, licked or sucked by his partner. Despite the name, it doesn't involve blowing. When it comes to oral sex for women, you might also hear people talk about 'cunnilingus' – which means stimulation of the vagina and clitoris using the mouth and tongue. Oral sex can be a big turn on for both partners, but it is just one aspect of sex, and not for everyone. It involves a great deal of communication, trust, respect and consent to make it meaningful – not to mention a squeaky clean soldier if you happen to be on the receiving end.

"My brother says he didn't enjoy his first blow job because his girlfriend went down on him before he was ready."
Danny, 16

Q: How do you have sex, exactly?

A: Sexual intercourse, or penetration, happens when the erect penis enters the vagina. The couple then move their bodies in a way that feels good for them both, generally by thrusting their hips to increase the level of sexual contact.

This kind of love-action can lead to orgasm and ejaculation (so be sure you've rolled on a condom just as soon as you get an erection). Penetration is just one part of sex, however, and by no means compulsory.

"I love being with my boyfriend, just touching and kissing."
Sara, 18

You might hear people talk about 'screwing', 'fucking' or 'shagging', along with a lot of macho nonsense about 'performing', but sex isn't a sport – it's a means of making babies, and an intimate expression of love and affection. There are no guarantees that sex will be great every time, but you're less likely to run into problems if there's a decent level of communication, trust and honesty between you. So if you want to be a man about it, and invite some respect from your partner, don't rush into sex for its own sake. Make it safe, and be sussed about contraception, but also make it mean something on both a physical and an emotional level.

"My first time was a nightmare. There's so much hype surrounding sex that you think it's going to be this huge event, but in the end it was messy and over really quickly. It was only when I met my current girlfriend that things started to improve. I guess there's no substitute for practice, but it also helps to be with someone you care about."
Dean, 19

Q: Does sex hurt?

A: First time intercourse can cause some discomfort for girls because there is a fragile membrane inside the vagina called the hymen that can stretch and/or break on penetration. An unbroken hymen used to be thought of as a symbol of virginity, but the fact is it usually breaks before first intercourse – through stuff like sport or using tampons. Lack of lubrication can also make sex less than enjoyable. This may be because you've steamed in without properly stimulating your partner and/or she's feeling nervous – which can make the vagina go into spasm.

Either way, it's important to stop if sex is painful for either of you. Slowing things down can make things more comfortable, as can extra lubrication. Make sure you use a water-based lubricant, such as KY Jelly, which can be safely used with a condom, unlike oil-based lubricants like Vaseline or baby lotion, which may damage the latex used to make condoms. You'll find a range of lubricants at the chemist. But nothing beats putting sex on hold and talking it over with your partner. It can only help you feel more at ease with each other, and give you both a better understanding of how to make sex a pleasurable part of your relationship.

The bottom line is sex shouldn't hurt, so if it continues to be a problem then see your doctor. They can check for any local infection that could be causing discomfort, plus it'll give you a chance to talk about contraception and safer sex.

"I still talk to my ex boyfriend about sex, simply because I got so used to being honest and upfront with him."
Lisa, 19

Q: What's anal sex?

A: It's the same as vaginal sex, except the penis penetrates the anus. Anal sex is often associated with gay lovemaking, but it's not for exclusively a gay thing – some straight couples do it because they like the physical sensation and feeling of intimacy it can bring. However, a lot of men and women don't find anal sex very appealing for religious and moral reasons, or just because they don't fancy it. There are also some health issues. The anus isn't really designed for penetration, and with no natural lubrication, the thin tissues tear very easily. This means it carries a very significant risk of sexually transmitted infection. Lovers who do find anal sex enjoyable should use a thick condom with a water-based lubricant like KY jelly (available without prescription from the chemist).

Anal sex is legal in the UK between consenting adults (gay or straight) who are over the age of consent, i.e. at least 16 years of age (17 in Northern Ireland).

SEX PROBLEMS:

Coming too soon

Up to 40% of men suffer at some stage from premature ejaculation, which means climaxing too soon during sex. Some experts say "premature" means ejaculation within two minutes of penetration. Others define it as being when a persistently early showdown causes grief within a sexual relationship.

Either way, here's how to stop your whistle blowing too soon and even last long into extra time:

Recognise the cause. Anxiety, stress, medication and sexual inexperience can all play a part. Learning to recognise and control the sensations in the penis can slow things down.

Don't despair. Almost all lads lack total control when they first start having sex or begin a new relationship. Generally it's just a sign of being really turned on, and experience will usually stop you frothing over too swiftly.

Learn to relax. Fretting about coming too quickly makes actually it more likely to happen. Taking your mind off the end result can help, though focusing on dull, non-sexual thoughts can also lessen your enjoyment in bed.

More foreplay. Removing sex from the agenda can often help take the pressure off, and ultimately delay orgasm.

The stop-start technique. An exercise designed to hold your level of arousal as you reach the point of no return. Masturbation can help you get a grip here. Simply slow down your love-action as you feel the onset of orgasm, or take a break completely, and you'll soon learn to control the sensations leading to orgasm.

The squeeze technique. Just before climax, grip your knob below the head and gently squeeze for about five seconds – not so your eyes water, but enough to make the sensations fade.

Thicker condoms. This can reduce the intensity of arousal leading up to climax.

Consult your doctor. Some physical conditions are related to premature ejaculation, including multiple sclerosis, diabetes, and spinal cord injuries. In this situation, medical treatment is the best course of action. Just be aware that for teen lads, 99% of ejaculatory problems are psychological in nature.

If you're delivering the goods too quickly, then chances are you can put this down to enthusiasm – and things will soon settle with experience. Even so, if you're worried in any way then talk it over with your doc. Male or female, it's a standard subject for them. In fact, you'll find it's no different from discussing the performance of your favourite football team – even if they haven't scored in a while.

SEX PROBLEMS:
Getting it up

Impotence is the proper name for problems in achieving an erection or keeping it up during sex. There can be lots of different causes, physical and psychological. The prospect of not getting a hard on for sex, or losing it midway through, is one of those things that strikes fear into the heart of any lad – but don't buy into pricey lotions, potions, pills and penis pumps. First, check out the XY DIY guide to sorting the problem.

Regaining control

● *For many impotence sufferers, no obvious cause is evident. Among lads with little experience of sexual intimacy, however, anxiety and worry can often be responsible.*

● *Ultimately, if you can get an erection through masturbation then chances are things will improve as you learn to feel more relaxed about sex.*

- If you're in a sexual relationship, aim to be open and honest about the issue. Bottle things up and you're more likely to make it into a much bigger deal than it really is. If your partner is understanding, you'll be more likely to relax and achieve an erection.

- Cutting out alcohol, tobacco and recreational drugs can often lead to significant improvements.

- If you're waking up with an erection (or 'morning glory' – see page 22), then rest easy. Even if it's not happening when you want it to, an 'early riser' proves there are no physical problems, and the cause is purely psychological.

- If the problem persists, don't hesitate to see your doctor, just to check there's no underlying medical reason.

9. head check

"Sometimes I feel so down I can't face getting out of bed."
Ajit, 15

"When my dad died, I just felt numb for months."
Phillip, 16

"I used to dread switching out the lights at night, because I knew I'd just lie there and worry. Then I started talking about it with my sister, and now I get the full eight hours!"
Dan, 13

WHERE'S YOUR HEAD AT?

People often say the toughest thing about being male is our inability to express emotions. It's a fair point. Let's face it, most of us tend not to cry freely, but claim instead to have 'something in our eye'! This tough outer shell is often kept in place by misguided manly ideals about coping with any kind of grief, stress, doubt or pressure. The trouble is we can't really enjoy life unless we're honest about what's going on in our heads.

"If I think I'm going to cry, I go to my room and lock the door."
Sean, 15

Everyone is different, and some lads do grow up feeling comfortable about expressing themselves, especially when they feel stressed out or troubled. They understand that it's not an admission of weakness to admit when they're not coping well. Yet clearly there are many others who suffer in silence for precisely this reason – often with tragic consequences. In the early eighties, suicide among the young male population has doubled. When things get tough for boys, it seems that half the battle is knowing how to ask for help.

One way of changing all that is by learning how to recognise the problems before they get out hand. Here are some of the biggest issues that could mess with your mindset, plus smart steps to keep on top of things.

STRESS

Feeling frazzled, or even close to cracking? Check out the Unzipped guide to stress management.

● *Stress is a natural response to difficult or threatening situations. It's designed to keep us out of trouble, by priming the 'fight or flight' response.*

- This involves the release of a natural chemical in the body called adrenaline. It makes your heart beat faster and switches the brain into a state of alert.

- Ideally, stress motivates you to deal with the situation but sometimes it can threaten to overwhelm.

- Feeling stressed out can leave you tense, irritable and helpless. It's even associated with headaches and other health problems, but it doesn't have to be this way ...

"I went through a stage where the slightest hassle used to leave me feeling tense and angry. My dad had just left home at the time, but it wasn't until I started talking about it to Mum that things started to make sense."
Ryan, 15

Deal with it:

- **Be positive.** Stress can work in your favour. When managed properly, it serves to keep you on your toes and motivates you to make important decisions.

- **Relax.** Managing stress can take some time, but it's important to face it calmly. Next time you feel under pressure, take a step away from the situation, breathe slowly and ask what's really giving you cause for concern. Chances are it won't seem so bad this way.

- **Be realistic.** Often people feel they can't cope when there's so much to be done. The trick is to take one step at a time in working towards your goal, rather *than viewing the stressful situation as a whole and freaking out.*

- **You're not alone.** *Ask whether you can honestly cope with things on your own. If not, then seek help. Often, just talking about the issue will help you find a way to overcome it.*

- **Exercise regularly.** *It'll help burn off excess adrenaline, as well as leaving you feeling less twitchy and more positive about yourself.*

"I always get a bit uptight before my exams, but at least it inspires me to sit down and work out a decent revision plan."
Bob, 15

DEPRESSION

Find yourself on a daily downer? Here's how to beat the blues:

- *Depression affects one in four people at some stage in their lives, with men counting for 34% of all cases. Teens are often thought to be most vulnerable.*

- *Sufferers feel hopelessly sad. Other symptoms include fatigue, sleeping problems, irritability and weight change (loss or gain – from decreased appetite and interest in food, or from comfort eating).*

- *Depression can be caused by factors like bereavement, stress and relationship difficulties, or internal problems* linked to hormone imbalance, changes in brain chemistry or blood sugar levels.

- Two out of three people with depression also lose interest in sex.

- Depression usually lasts between three months and two years. Ninety per cent of cases are successfully treated with some therapy, or therapy plus medication.

"Feeling sad, day after day, almost did my head in."
Anthony, 15

Deal with it:

- ***Talk about it.*** *If you're feeling down, and it's affecting your daily life, then don't be afraid to open up about it. Depression is a treatable condition, and voicing your feelings to friends and family is a good first step towards recovery.*

- ***Relaxation techniques.*** *Stuff like yoga, meditation and massage can help beat the stress and anxiety often linked to depression. Even exercise like swimming, jogging or football can make you feel better, but don't rely on it as your only form of treatment.*

- **Review your lifestyle.** Perhaps you're feeling overstretched with schoolwork or exam revision, or turning to ciggies, drink and drugs as a means of escape. Take a good look at the way you live your life, and see if there's room for improvement.

- **See your doctor.** He or she is trained to deal with depression, and can draw on a range of effective therapies – not just medication but ...

- **Counselling.** Talking to a trained counsellor is an effective means of getting to grips with the root of your depression. Your doctor can recommend a psychotherapist or self-help group.

"Learning that depression was an illness gave me hope. For me, it meant people understood what I was going through, and could help me get better."
Lawrence, 17

Suicidal thoughts

I've made a mess of my life, and it's all too much for me. I can't talk to my family about it, because they just think I'm trouble, and I'm starting to think the simple solution would be to kill myself.
Darren, 15

Unzipped advice:

Whatever you're feeling right now, suicide is never the answer. It would destroy not only your life, but also those of people who care for you – and that includes your family. Ultimately, there is no problem that can't be sorted, so please don't despair. Instead, make this the moment you regain control. All you have to do is accept that there are people and places that can help you get back on your feet. If you feel unable to take this to your family, or confide in a good friend, then call The Samaritans (0345 909090). Trained counsellors are on hand 24 hours a day who can provide confidential emotional support, and help you identify positive ways to deal with the situation.

Just by talking through your problems, you'll find it easier to get things in perspective. Whatever it is that's made you feel so low, you don't have to deal with it alone. Help is out there. It's just a question of asking.

Crime blues

"Recently I was mugged by a gang of lads. They threatened me with a knife and stole my mobile

phone, and it's really shaken me up. I'm too ashamed to tell anyone, because they were younger than me, but I can't sleep and I feel scared when I'm out on my own."
Ross, 15

Unzipped advice:

Whatever you're feeling right now is a perfectly natural response to a traumatic event. We all react in different ways to crime, and go through anything from shock to anger, fear and depression. Young men are increasingly finding themselves victims of crime, but bottling things up won't help restore your confidence.

Begin by reporting what happened to the police. If it helps, confide in a trusted friend or family member and ask them to come with you. Involving the law could mean these lads are brought to justice before they put someone else through the same grief you're going through. At the same time, you need to open up about your feelings in order to make sense of them. If you feel unable to talk to someone you know, call Victim Support on 0845 3030900. Please don't feel ashamed of the fact that these lads were younger than you. Under threat of violence, you were absolutely right to give them what they wanted, and people will respect you for that. But now it's time to stand up for yourself by reporting the incident and working to move on. If you allow the experience to take away your enjoyment of life, they'll have robbed you on two counts.

Still choked up

"My best friend died a few years ago, but whenever I think about it I feel like crying. Nobody else still seems to be cut up about it, so why me?"
Ted, 16

Unzipped advice:

Grief affects everyone in different ways, and over different periods of time. Coming to terms with the loss of someone who played a big part in your life is one of the toughest emotional challenges you'll face. People will understand, however, and it always helps to talk it through with someone who identifies with your loss.

Chances are your mates still have wobbly moments, but you won't find out unless you ask. It takes courage to open up about such private feelings for the first time, but once you start it will get easier.

If you feel uncomfortable raising the subject with a friend, call Cruse Bereavement Care (0870 167 1677) and talk it over with a trained bereavement counsellor. Whatever you're feeling is fine, just be aware that you don't have to deal with it alone. In time, and with support and understanding, your loss will become more bearable and allow you to move on with your life.

SELF-ESTEEM

The way you think about yourself (often called self-esteem) has a big influence on the way you live your life, and also how others see you. There are many different causes of low self-esteem, ranging from your family background to depression or bullying. Whatever your experience, don't do yourself down any more.

Spot the symptoms

- *Disappointment about your achievements*
- *Lack of confidence*
- *Shyness in social situations*
- *Being quick to lose your temper and/or blame others*
- *Reluctance to take on new challenges, because you think you'll fail.*

"I hate it when I go red. As soon as my cheeks warm up, I try to turn the attention onto someone else."
Tim, 15

Deal with it:

- ***Pinpoint the positive.*** *Identify one good thing about yourself that other people like and admire – it doesn't have to be a big deal, perhaps your sense of humour – and then build on it! You'll soon find a good response from others will help you feel better about yourself.*

- **Review your attitude.** *Try not to do yourself down when people show an interest in your life. Instead of moaning about the way things are going, come up with something good that's happened lately and share it. In short, think of your glass as half full, not half empty!*

- **Learn from mistakes.** *Let's face it, we all screw up sometimes. It's human nature, but blaming yourself won't make things better. The best thing you can do is learn from the experience and move on having gained something positive.*

- **Be assertive.** *It's common for people with low self-esteem to react badly when they're feeling under threat, and go on the attack. Quite often, this can take the form of bullying, which makes other people feel small so you can feel big. The way forward is to be assertive instead of aggressive. This means being positive about all the good things you have to offer, rather than looking for the negative in others. Keep calm at all times, be nice, and don't act without first thinking about the consequences. Treat other people with the respect you expect from them, and you'll soon make your presence known for all the right reasons!*

"I used to be really shy with people, but then I started to resent the way it ruled my life. Nowadays I just go for it, and I've made so many more good friends as a result."
Barry, 14

SLEEP PROBLEMS

Sleep is the time when growth hormones really kick in and much of the body's repair work is carried out. Too little can weaken your immune system, and stop your mind from functioning properly. Even so, that doesn't stop a lot of stressed out lads from losing out on vital downtime. Here's your dream ticket.

- **Work out what you need.** *Between five and nine hours is average, but sussing out what's good for you means waking up naturally for a while. Why? Because sleep runs in cycles. Our biological clock tells us when we're tired, and wakes us when we've had enough.*

- **Go to bed at the same time.** *Once you've worked out how much sleep you need, think about what time you have to be up in the morning, and calculate the best time to turn in. After a while, your body will soon know when it can switch off for the night, which means you're less likely to wind up lying in bed staring at the ceiling for hours on end.*

- **Get up when you wake up.** *If you happen to stir before your alarm then get out of bed. Obeying your body clock might be a chore but you'll feel more alert through the day.*

"I got into such a habit of not sleeping that I was scared to go to bed. I knew I'd lie there worrying about school."
Lloyd, 13

- **Sort your stress.** *Personal problems can often seem worse last thing at night, and this can stop you from sleeping. Talking things through with someone you trust can get things in perspective, or ask your doctor to recommend a course of counselling.*

- **Shape up.** *Regular work-outs reduce sleep-stopping adrenaline. Exercise also drinks up excess energy that could leave you with your sheets in a tangle. Just make sure you give yourself plenty of winding-down time before you turn in, otherwise all that adrenaline will keep you awake!*

"I don't lie in any more, because it stops me from sleeping properly at night."
Martyn, 15

- **Avoid cigarettes and coffee.** *Stimulants guaranteed to keep you awake.*

- **Lose the booze.** *A drink may help you doze off, but alcohol dehydrates the body during slumber and leads to disturbed sleep.*

- **Eat properly.** *Avoid eating lots last thing at night or going to bed hungry. If you're stuffed or starving, your stomach won't let you rest.*

- **Check your bed.** *Sleep experts recommend a firm, level and supported mattress. If your bed is sagging, a sheet of plywood underneath it should provide the support you need.*

10. thrills and spills

"I used to think getting really drunk in town on a Saturday was a right laugh. But one time I woke up the next day and I couldn't remember where I'd been or what I'd done, and that scared me. I like to enjoy myself, but no good comes from being out of control."
Lee, 15

"I love playing video games. It gives me a chance to unwind after finishing my homework. My sister says it's sad, but what does she know?"
Michael, 13

"Having a tattoo was a kick for a couple of months, but now it just feels like a hassle because I'm too scared to show my dad."
Stevie, 16

Your gags

What do men and beer bottles have in common?
They're both empty from the neck up!
Gary, 14

THE FACE OF TEMPTATION

We all want a good time, right? Whether you're bored with life or run ragged by it, the temptation to let off steam can be hard to resist. A knockabout with a ball, or an online shoot-'em-up session can be a blast. Some people say that boys get physical or resort to fantasy worlds as a substitute for talking through their troubles with someone they trust, but if it leaves you feeling freshened up to tackle the real issues afterwards then why not go with it?

"Things never seem so bad once I've been for a run. It helps me think."
Elliott, 15

But what if you take a good time too far, or turn to something as a way of blotting out your problems completely? There are plenty of ways to walk on the wild side, from drink to drugs and all out bad-lad behaviour, and if everyone else appears to be swaggering in that direction it can be hard to hang back – which is why it's so important to understand the facts surrounding each issue.

"My mates once shared a bottle of vodka mixed with a carton of orange juice. They gave me grief for not joining in, but I knew exactly how bad it was going to leave them feeling."
Sol, 15

This is the bit where you'll find hard info on some of the major temptations facing lads today – not just ways to get out of it, but habits you might fall into such as smoking or gambling that could have an impact on your long term welfare. That's followed up in the next chapter by the ultimate lowdown on drugs – from the effects to the risks involved. Nobody can tell you how to lead your life, but you owe it to yourself to understand the risks behind the appeal. That way, you'll feel more confident about making informed decisions. It has to be better than just going for it and hoping for the best.
Knowledge is power, after all, but ignorance is no excuse.

SMOKING

"I find smoking a real turn off. Kissing a guy with ashtray breath? Yik."
Sara, 15

- *The shredded brown stuff inside a cigarette is called tobacco. It's basically a leaf from the tobacco plant that has been dried, chopped up and processed.*

- *Tobacco smoke contains about 4000 chemicals, many of which are harmful to your health.*

- *Tobacco also contains a stimulant drug called nicotine, which plays a big part in keeping smokers coming back for more.*

The score with the law

From October 2007, if you're under 18 it is illegal for a shopkeeper to sell you cigarettes, while the police can confiscate your smoking gear if you're caught puffing away in public.

What's the draw?

People are tempted to light up for all kinds of reasons, and every smoker will give you a different answer. Here are some of the main contenders:

The smoking lifestyle. Lighting up is often viewed as an act of rebellion and even sophistication. It's a strong image that has long been manipulated by the cigarette industry and the media to reinforce certain ideas, attitudes and beliefs. All too often, lads think of smoking as shorthand for cool, which is to forget that it's also a shortcut to health and wealth problems.

Joining the pack. Peer pressure can be a powerful force, which means if your mates are lighting up then you might find it hard to resist. Much depends on your self-esteem, so if you feel confident in yourself and the image you give out, then you're less likely to light up because you're worried about feeling like the odd one out.

Your background. Growing up in a smoky environment plays a big role in shaping your attitude. Although some lads react against it, others who fall into the habit are statistically more likely to become big time smokers.

Mood control. Nicotine in tobacco is a powerful and fast acting drug that has a stimulating effect on the body. Even so, many people believe that reaching for the cigarettes actually helps keep them stay calm, relieving stress and feelings of nervousness. There's no doubt that people smoke because they enjoy it, but while the act of puffing on a smoke might distract them mentally, the physical changes actually work against them.

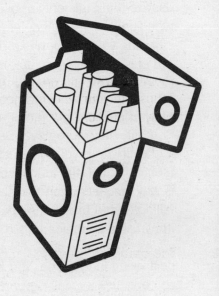

The addiction factor. Experts continue to argue about whether nicotine should be classified as a physically addictive substance. Despite this, the majority of smokers will tell you how easy it is to get mentally hooked on the habit. This is because it's possible to become psychologically dependent on anything you do on a regular basis to change your mood. When it comes to cigarettes, this means you keep lighting up because you feel that you can't manage without a smoke. Just be aware that becoming dependent on cigarettes doesn't happen overnight. Often, the problem only becomes apparent when you realise you can't stop.

Risk rundown

Everyone knows that smoking is harmful to health, but it's easy to think this only applies to wheezing old codgers who should've stopped years ago. The fact is every cigarette you smoke has a damaging effect on your body, not to mention your wallet and even your pulling potential. Here are the main offenders:

Lung disease. Your lungs are designed to extract oxygen from air. They were never built to handle cigarette smoke, and every drag you take makes its mark. The irritants in tobacco attack the lungs' self-cleaning mechanism, which is why smokers often find themselves hawking up gunk, or falling foul to bronchitis (aka smokers' cough). Another irreversible condition called emphysema kicks in later in a smoker's life, and slowly reduces breathing capacity by destroying lung tissue. You may not notice it to begin, as you only use a small proportion of your lungs to breathe, but the damage is permanent and can kill.

Cancer and heart trouble. Cigarette smoke is carcinogenic, which means anything it touches within the body increases the chances of cancer kicking in. So it's not just your lungs that are at risk, but your mouth, nose, tongue, blood, pancreas and kidneys. Smokers also increase the risk of wrecking their tickers, with tobacco being linked to 80% of all heart attacks in men under the age of 45.

Cash flow considerations. Cigarettes aren't cheap, and if you're supporting a steady habit it can cost more than your health. In a week, the money shelled out on a ten-a-day habit could easily buy a full-price CD, while a year-long smoke supply would cost you more than a brand new DVD player, and a TV thrown in to watch it on.

Bad breath blues. Tobacco smoke dries out membranes inside the mouth that are responsible for producing bacteria-beating saliva. As a result, all kinds of bugs begin to fester and rot inside your gob. It can be hard to detect nasty niffs on your own breath, of course, but if people begin to back away whenever you speak, it might be time to ask what kind of vibe this ciggie habit is really giving off.

'Wood' problems. Cigarette smoking is known to restrict blood flow to the penis, which means blokes who smoke are at risk of impotence (difficulties in getting an erection and keeping it up). Recent studies suggest that up to 120,000 UK men have already made themselves impotent through smoking.

Sperm suffering. So having kids is probably the last thing on your mind right now, but lighting up now can badly compromise your chances of becoming a dad later in life. Why? Because nicotine knackers up your sperm quality and quantity. Simple as that.

Help yourself!

Kicking the habit takes guts, but it's also the greatest thing you'll ever do for your body. Stay smoke-free and you can be sure you'll be proud of your achievement. Every day people give up smoking in a way that works for them, but ultimately it takes willpower. Here are some quick fix tips:

● *Make a date to stop smoking and stick to it.*

● *Steer clear of situations where you're tempted to light up, like walking home from school with mates, or nipping out to post a letter!*

● *Chewing gum can help keep the craving at bay (anything that keeps your mouth or hands occupied).*

● *Fill your time creatively. Exercise can help beat the craving, and can only help restore your body to its former glory!*

● *Remember that every day you go without a smoke you're beating the addiction.*

Smoking stopwatch

Your body benefits from being smoke-free just seconds after you've stubbed out your final smoke. Time your achievement, right here:

After:

● **20 mins** – *your blood pressure drops back to normal levels*

● **2 days** – *there's no more nicotine left in your body*

- **3 to 9 months** – *you can take in 10% more air into your lungs*

- **5 months** – *your risk of a heart attack is 50% less than a smoker*

- **10 years** – *your chances of a heart attack falls to the same as someone who has never lit up.*

Lifeline: For advice and support to help stop smoking call QUITLINE on 0800 00 22 00

DRINKING

"I got roped into playing a drinking game at a party once. I knew my limit, so I quit after a couple of rounds. It was a bit humiliating, but not like it was for the winner. He ended up puking in the garden for the rest of the evening!"
Shane, 15

- *Alcohol is produced by fermenting fruits, vegetables or grains. It's found in drinks like beer, lager, alcopops, cider, wine and spirits such as rum, vodka and whiskey.*

- *In small amounts, alcohol can help people to relax and feel sociable. In increasing quantities, speech can become slurred, co-ordination affected and emotions heightened. Go beyond your limits and you risk spinning out, vomiting, unconsciousness, coma and even death.*

- *The effect depends on the strength of the drink (measured as a % volume) and how fast it is consumed. It also depends on when the drinker last ate, his weight, mood and surroundings.*

- *Tolerance can develop among regular drinkers, which means you need more to get the same effect. This can be dangerous as you may wind up accidentally drinking more than your body can handle, resulting in overdose.*

The score with the law

It is illegal for anyone under the age of 18 to buy alcohol. You're allowed to drink at home under this age, but police have the power to confiscate your alcohol if you're boozing in public, and contact your parents too.

What's the draw?

Alcohol plays a big part in our world, with over 90% of the adult population enjoying a drink on a regular basis. That doesn't make it compulsory to crack open a six-pack, but understanding the reasons for the appeal could help you drink sensibly – if that's what you choose to do.

Curiosity. Drink is big business. With the alcohol industry spending more than £200 million on promoting its products in every shape or form, it's no wonder that we become aware of booze from a very early age. So when the opportunity arises to try it for ourselves, the temptation can be hard to resist. Some lads find their parents are the first to let them try a taste, as this gives them more control over the situation. For many others, however, it's peer pressure that persuades them to give it a go – often before they've learned to respect alcohol.

The buzz. Like any drug, alcohol affects your mood. In small amounts it can help people loosen up, so they feel chatty and less self-conscious. The problems only kick in if you turn to drink because it seems like the only way to have a good time, or because you're uptight, bored, or lacking the self-confidence to just be yourself when sober.

The image. OK, so hard drinking has a macho appeal. We're led to believe that a real man can drink without dropping, while our action movie heroes are often seen steadying their nerves with a drop of the strong stuff. In reality, if you drink to get drunk, the end result is always the same. You might have a good time up to a point, but after that you risk spinning out, vomiting or just doing something you badly regret. It doesn't impress, and nor will it leave you feeling good about yourself. Inside every 'hard drinker' you'll find an individual with personal problems he can't sort out because booze has got the better of him.

Risk rundown

Drinking too much doesn't just leave you with a hangover. The fact is alcohol has an impact on your health, and that means your mind as well as your body.

Bad skin. Drinking deprives your skin of vital nutrients, and can also dry it out. The result? Spots and early wrinkles.

Liver trouble. Alcohol in the body is processed by your liver. Like any engine, your body risks a breakdown if you thrash it, and a heavy drinking habit can leave you prone to stomach bleeding, fatty liver and a condition called cirrhosis – where your liver cells gradually give up the ghost and turn to scar tissue. Quitting drink early enough might halt the disease, but leave it too late and it can be fatal.

Mental health problems. A heavy drinking habit in your teen years can affect brain development involved in learning and memory. Alcohol is also closely related to mental problems such as depression, so if you're prone to feeling blue then booze will only leave you feeling worse. It's even been estimated that alcohol is involved in about 80% of all suicide attempts in the UK.

Beer bellies. Alcoholic drinks tend to have high sugar content. A couple of pints every evening may not seem like much, but it could pack on an extra quarter to your recommended calorie intake. Not only can this result in weight gain all over, guys risk developing a beer gut – or beer belly – a term used to describe a build-up of fat in and around the abdominal area. Up to 40% of all blokes are likely to blob out here, and it's almost certainly fuelled by a couch potato lifestyle that involves boozing on a regular basis.

Brewer's droop. Drinking may boost your confidence when it comes to chatting people up, but it also serves to dull the sensory nerve transmissions from your brain to your boxer shorts. Even a pint can affect your performance, and stop you from achieving maximum erection potential. 'Brewer's droop' (as it's often called) can be a bit embarrassing, but heavy long-term drinking is also linked to serious problems such as reduced testosterone levels and infertility.

Violent behaviour. Alcohol is known to muck up your judgement. People are less likely to hold back when they've been drinking, which can spell trouble, whether you're swinging that punch or unlucky enough to be on the receiving end. The fact is drunken violence is linked to 76,000 facial injuries in the UK each year, with the majority of incidents taking place in or near licensed premises such as pubs, bars and off licences.

Help yourself!

Drinking isn't compulsory. You can choose not to booze, if not all the time then every now and then, and if your mates have any respect for you they'll rate your sense of independence. Either way, being smart about alcohol means thinking ahead. Here are some tips to be sure that alcohol doesn't get the better of you:

- *Eat a decent meal before you go out.* Starchy stuff like bread, potatoes and pasta, and fatty food such as chips can take a while to digest and will help absorb alcohol.

- *Know your limit.* Don't set out to drink up to the amount of alcohol your body can tolerate. Instead, aim to enjoy a drink as part of the social setting, but to respect your limits. If you're not sure what you can handle, take it very easy indeed. You'll soon get an idea of where to draw the (drink) line.

- **Pace yourself.** *Give your body a chance to process the alcohol from one drink to the next. Also sip each drink instead of swigging it down. It'll give you greater control, and reduce the risk of embarrassing yourself in front of everyone.*

- **Alternate alcohol with water.** *Keep up the fluids that matter by switching to a non-alcoholic, non-fizzy drink every now and then.*

- **Avoid mixing drinks.** *Your body won't thank you for sending down different types of booze. It means more toxins to deal with, while the different alcohol levels make the overall effects unpredictable. As a result, you may find you stop enjoying yourself, and start wishing you hadn't had that last drink.*

Hangover help

Nobody likes feeling hungover (the result of drinking too much). The combined effects of being dehydrated by alcohol and having toxins swim about your system can be responsible for anything from headaches and nausea to

fatigue and diarrhoea. So, if you're going to drink then at least think about whether you can cope with the consequences. And if you do wake up wishing you hadn't drunk so much, here are some steps you can take to minimise the pain and suffering:

- ***Keep sipping water or juice.*** *But avoid fizzy drinks. This is because if there's any alcohol left in your body the carbonated bubbles will only stir it up!*

- ***Steer clear of coffee.*** *Many people with a hangover drink coffee because it helps them feel more alert. The trouble is that caffeine also serves to dehydrate your body further, which could leave you feeling worse.*

- ***Eat something.*** *Even though a hangover can take away your appetite, eating will help restore the glucose levels your body needs to feel good again. Stick to easily digestible stuff like toast and cereals. Even if you can't manage much, keep eating little and often.*

- ***Drink rethink.*** *If hangovers are becoming a regular feature in your life, take time out to review your relationship with alcohol. There's a fine line between enjoying a drink and letting booze control you. If you think you may have crossed it, aim to recognise the problem and accept that you may need help to sort it.*

Lifeline: If you feel able to talk about alcohol with your parents or carer, it can only help bring the issue into the open and establish a better understanding between you. Alternatively, if you'd prefer to seek confidential support and advice about your own drinking or somebody else's, call DrinkLine (0800 917 8282) and talk in confidence to a trained counsellor.

TATTOOING AND BODY PIERCING

"When he was a lad, my dad had both ears pierced. He doesn't wear anything in them any more, but you can still see the holes and everyone winds him up about it!"
Tim, 12

- *A tattoo is a permanent design using coloured ink pigment punctured deep into the skin.*

- *Body piercing is another bold personal statement that sends out strong messages to the world around. Popular piercing targets include ears, nose, eyebrow, lip, nipples and genitals.*

The score with the law

It is illegal to be tattooed unless you're over 18. To avoid the risk of infections like tetanus or even HIV, tattoos must be performed under totally hygienic conditions by a professional – which means they'll insist on proof of your age first. Although there is no legislation controlling body piercing, some practitioners are regulated by their local authority. This means they must respect certain standards in order to receive an official certificate.

What's the draw?

Many people consider tattooing and piercing to be an uplifting ritual that transforms the body into a work of art. The process is painful, but many people who have been through it feel this makes the end result seem even more meaningful.

Risk rundown

Tattooing. Tattoos are permanent. They might fade and blur, but they won't go away. Even if you fool a tattooist into thinking you're old enough, consider all the people you'll have to face afterwards. Removal is possible with laser treatment, but this is expensive, can be painful and doesn't work for all tattoos.

Body piercing. Until proper regulation comes into force, you could be risking your health by getting holey. Body piercing is a skill that requires both training and experience. Without it, you risk serious infection and other complications. Sure, you can remove the jewellery if you grow bored of it, but the hole will always be visible.

Body art – the alternative. If you're serious about body piercing or tattooing, why not try something short-term first? Temporary tattoos (either henna or transfers) and clip on body jewellery are easily available nowadays. That way, you can give it a go, with no harm done if you're not totally sold on the idea.

GAMBLING

"Playing scratch cards is a buzz. My mate and me always buy one if we can afford it, and dream about what we'll do with the money if we win. The most I've ever made is £10, but I've spent far more than that."
Alex, 15

● *People gamble (place money, or 'a bet') on the outcome of almost any activity or event.*

● *Gambling takes many forms, from fruit machines to horse and greyhound racing, online casinos and lottery games, even the chance of snow falling on Christmas Day!*

● *Research has shown that men are twice as likely as women to be serious gamblers.*

● *A recent study showed that 5% of young people under 16 had a gambling problem, while 2% were obsessed with scratch cards.*

The score with the law

UK law states that it is illegal for anyone under the age of 16 to buy scratch cards or lottery tickets. In addition, you must be 18 or over to bet in a licenced betting shop. The same age restriction applies to playing slot/fruit machines offering cash prizes of £10 or more (except in Northern Ireland which has no lower age limit).

What's the draw?

Gambling always starts out as a bit of fun, and often appeals to young men. The element of risk and the chance to make fast money have a macho appeal that can be hard to resist. In reality, most people lose cash while the gambling industry

continues to clean up. So if you're going to play, set a limit on the money you plan to shell out before you start. That way, you're less likely to get carried away.

Risk rundown

Gambling lifts blood pressure, heart rate and adrenalin levels – and this gives an instant hit. The buzz comes from thinking that you might win, rather than the money itself, and problems can set in if you become dependent on that kick.

The odds of winning:

- *To win £8 on a fruit machine: 600/1*
- *£50,000 scratchcard jackpot: 2.57 million/1*
- *Top prize on the lottery: 14.5 million/1*
- *Football pools: 7.5 million/1*

Lifeline: If you're concerned about your own gambling habit, or think a friend or parent is gambling too much, call Gamblers Anonymous for confidential information, advice or counselling. The number is 0207 384 3040.

10. drugs: the lowdown

"I wanted to talk to my dad about ecstasy, because I didn't understand why some people have died after taking it. As soon as I raised the subject, he freaked out and kept asking me why I was so interested in knowing. In the end I just asked my mates, the trouble is I don't believe everything they tell me."
Kris, 14

When it comes to drugs, everyone seems to have an opinion, and emotions often run high. As a result, the facts can sometimes get lost in the argument, and myths are reinforced. It doesn't help that drugs appeal to some lads in the same way as drinking, and that 'getting off your face' to show how supposedly crazy you are is somehow a mark of a real man. The truth is there are serious risks associated with drug taking, so it's vital you have access to info you can trust – not just about the highs but the lows and the law involved.

Different drugs have different effects. Even so, some work in similar ways and can be divided into broad categories:

STIMULANTS
Drugs that act on the central nervous system and increase brain activity: speed, ecstasy, cocaine/crack, poppers.

DEPRESSANTS
Drugs that act on the central nervous system and slow down brain activity: alcohol, tranquillisers, gases, aerosols and glue.

HALLUCINOGENS
Drugs that act on the mind, distorting the way users see and hear things: LSD (acid), magic mushrooms, cannabis, ketamine.

ANALGESICS
Drugs that have a painkilling effect and which can also bring on feelings of warmth and contentment: heroin, morphine.

- *It's impossible to accurately predict the effects of any drug. Much depends on the quantity taken, the user's mood, physical health and state of mind, and where they are at the time.*

The score with the law

Drugs laws are complex, but ignorance is no defence.
If the police believe you're carrying drugs they can search
you. If they find something, and you're under 14, then your
parent/s or carer will be told, and if it's your second
offence then you could wind up in a youth court. If you're
14 or over, then you may be prosecuted under The Misuse
of Drugs Act 1971. This law divides drugs into three
different categories, each with different penalties. Here's
what you could face if you're caught possessing drugs or
supplying drugs to other people.

Class A: Heroin, cocaine, LSD, ecstasy, crack

Maximum penalties: seven years in prison and/or a fine for
possession, life and/or a fine for supply.

Class B: Speed (amphetamines)

Maximum penalties: five years in prison and/or a fine for
possession, 14 years and/or a fine for supply.

Class C: Cannabis, tranquillisers that haven't been
prescribed to you

Maximum penalties: two years in prison and/or a fine for
possession, five years in prison and/or a fine for supply.

Harm reduction

● *There's no such thing as a safe drug. The effects can sometimes be unexpected.*

● *Street drugs have often been mixed with other substances, so users can never be 100% sure of what they're taking.*

● *Mixing alcohol with other drugs can be seriously dangerous. This is because booze serves to slow down the nervous system (controlling heart and breathing rate). Combined with other depressant drugs, it could see the body shut down altogether.*

● *Ecstasy affects body temperature. Dancing for long periods in a hot environment like a club can cause users to overheat, and this can kill. Users should chill out regularly, and sip about a pint of non-alcoholic fluid such as water or fruit juice over the course of each hour.*

Addiction uncovered

OK, so you know that different drugs work in different ways. You understand that the effects depend on the amount you're doing, where you are at the time, and how you shape up in mind and body. But that doesn't mean you're too smart to get hooked. Here's why:

Addiction: A compulsion to keep using a particular substance to feel good or to avoid feeling bad.

Physical addiction: A dependency that develops through repeated use of a drug that changes body chemistry, e.g.

alcohol, heroin, tranquillisers. This means your body develops a hunger that you have to keep feeding.

Psychological addiction: This is a risk with any drug. Quite simply, the mind can get hooked on any substance that you keep using to feel a certain way. If drugs appeal to you as an escape, then you could be heading for dependency problems.

Withdrawal: Breaking a drug habit can be tough, and even life-threatening in cases of chronic addition to alcohol or tranquillisers. Even after your body's kicked a physical dependency, the mental cravings can be intense for a long time.

Recovery: This means sticking to the idea that you're better off without drugs, no matter how bad you feel. It can be hard to pull off on your own, but help is always out there.

Lifeline: If you're concerned about any drugs issue, and you want free and confidential information, advice, counselling, or even just a chat, call The National Drugs Helpline / Talk to Frank: 0800 77 66 00.

DRUGS: THE UNZIPPED FILES

There's no point preaching about drug dangers, because it isn't what you want to hear. It's down to you to form your own opinion, and you owe it to yourself to make it informed. So here are the facts about different drugs – stripped right down so the risks speak for themselves.

CANNABIS (marijuana, dope, blow, weed, hash, ganja)
Cannabis is a natural substance from a plant called hemp.
It comes in resin form (a dark, solid lump), or as
chopped-up leaves, stalks and seeds (called 'grass'). It can
be rolled with a tobacco in a 'spliff' or 'joint', smoked on its
own in a special pipe or eaten. Class C penalties apply.

The effects

- *Getting 'stoned' on cannabis makes most users relaxed and talkative.*

- *Colours, taste, and music can seem more appealing and intense.*

- *The physical effects include bloodshot eyes, increased appetite and, in some cases, dizziness. The effects can last several hours.*

The risks

- *Short-term memory and concentration is affected.*

- *It can make users paranoid and anxious, depending on their mood and surroundings.*

- *Cannabis impairs driving skills, so never get in a car with someone who is stoned.*

- *Long-term use can leave some people feeling like they can't relax and be sociable unless they're stoned.*

NITRITES (poppers, amyl, butyl)

Nitrites (commonly known as poppers) come in clear, liquid form and the vapour is inhaled for its effects. Possession is not illegal, but supply can be an offence.

The effects

Inhaling causes a sudden surge of blood to the heart and brain.

Users experience this as a very quick, intense 'head rush'.

The effects fade two to five minutes after use.

The risks

After the rush comes the headache.

Some users may feel faint and sick.

Regular use can cause skin problems around the mouth and nose.

Nitrites work by reducing blood pressure, and this makes it dangerous for people with anaemia, glaucoma, breathing or heart problems.

SPEED (amphetamines, billy, whizz, uppers, sulphate)
Speed usually comes as a dirty-white powder that is
snorted, swallowed, injected or smoked. It is believed to be
the most impure illegal drug in the UK, and can be cut
with anything from washing powder to chalk dust. Class B
penalties apply.

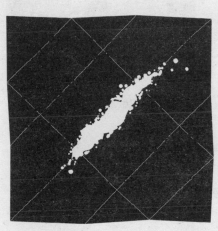

The effects
● *Speed is a stimulant.
It increases both
heart and breathing
rate.*

● *Users feel more lively
and confident. They
may become more
talkative too.*

● *Some users become
tense and anxious
while on speed.*

The risks
● *The comedown can last for a couple of days, leaving
users feeling wiped out and irritable.*

● *Tolerance for speed can build quickly, so bigger doses are
required for the same sort of hit.*

● *Heavy abuse over long periods has been linked to mental
illness, and can place a serious strain on the heart.*

ACID (LSD, trips, tabs, blotters, dots)
Class A drug that usually comes in tiny squares of paper (often with a picture printed on one side), that has been treated with the chemical Lysergic acid diethylamide – LSD for short.

The effects

● *Acid is a hallucinogen that has a strong effect on the mind.*

● *Users may experience a distorted sense of sight and sound, even time.*

● *The effects are known as 'a trip' and can last up to eight hours.*

● *Every trip is different, and influenced by the user's mood, their surroundings and the people they're with.*

The risks

● *A 'good' trip can't be guaranteed, while a bad trip is more likely if the user is anxious or nervous.*

● *A bad trip can be a very frightening experience – even for experienced users.*

● *Once the trip kicks in it can't be stopped until the effect of the drug has worn off. It can often leave users feeling very shaken for a long time afterwards.*

- *Using acid can complicate existing mental problems such as depression or anxiety.*

MAGIC MUSHROOMS ('shrooms, mushies, liberty cap)
A type of mushroom with hallucinogenic properties, that grows wild in many parts of the world, including the UK. Can be eaten raw, dried, or stewed into a tea. Many types look like magic mushrooms, however, but are in fact poisonous. When prepared (i.e. dried or stewed), magic mushrooms may be considered as a Class A drug.

The effects

- *Similar to acid, but the trip is generally milder.*

- *Users may feel giggly, and 'spaced out'.*

- *Much depends on the user's mood and expectations, their surroundings, and who they're with at the time.*

- *A trip may last 4–9 hours.*

The risks
- *Biggest risk is poisoning, due to picking the wrong kind of mushroom. In some cases this can be fatal.*

- *Magic mushrooms can cause stomach pains, vomiting and diarrhoea.*

133

If users feel sick, they should go straight to hospital, if possible with a sample of the mushroom they have taken.

Bad trips happen, and can be very frightening.

May complicate existing mental conditions.

ECSTASY (E, XTC, disco biscuits, MDMA, doves) Illegally manufactured but popular club culture drug. Usually comes in tablet form – often with a picture or logo on it. Ecstasy is a Class A drug.

The effects

Users can feel alert, and in tune with their surroundings as well the people they're with.

Heightened sense of sound, colour and emotion.

Stimulant effects may encourage users to dance for long periods of time.

Effects can last 3-6 hours.

The risks

The effects can be unpleasant when they first kick in, including nausea, sweating and a racing heart.

Different tablets contain different levels of MDMA, some may not contain any at all, while the substances used to cut (or bulk out) the drug may have unpredictable effects.

- Some users report bad experiences with ecstasy, including feelings of paranoia, panic and confusion.

- Ecstasy messes with the body's temperature controls. Users have been known to overheat and dehydrate due to dancing for long periods without keeping up non-alcoholic fluids (see page 127). In some cases, this can kill.

- The comedown can leave users feeling very low for some days.

- The long-term effects of ecstasy on the mind are not yet fully understood.

COCAINE (coke, charlie, chang, gack)
A white powder with powerful stimulant properties. Generally sniffed/snorted up the nose, though some users inject it. Cocaine is a Class A drug.

The effects

- Users enjoy a sense of well being and euphoria.

- Effects are intense, and last for 15-30 minutes.

- As the effects wear off, users may feel anxious, irritable and/or depressed.

- *Many feel the need to take more to delay this 'comedown' effect.*

The risks

- *Snorting cocaine irritates the nasal membranes. It can cause sneezing, congestion and nosebleeds.*

- *Persistent abuse can cause serious damage to the structure of the nose.*

- *Users may develop a strong psychological dependence, which means they get hooked on the euphoric feelings the drug brings.*

- *A cocaine habit can be expensive, and difficult to control.*

- *Tolerance builds, which means repeat users need more to get the same effect.*

- *Overdose is possible, and may be fatal.*

CRACK (rock, stone, wash)
A smokeable form of cocaine that comes in small lumps or 'rocks'. Crack is a Class A drug.

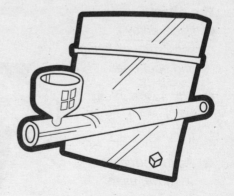

The effects

- *Similar to snorting cocaine. The euphoric effects are more intense, but fade after a few minutes.*

- *The feelings of anxiety, paranoia and irritability that follow often compel users to chase the high by repeating the dose.*

The risks

- *Crack is a highly addictive drug. A habit can quickly become out of control.*

- *Smoking crack can cause serious lung damage.*

- *Repeat users need more to get the same effect, increasing the risk of overdose.*

- *Heavy use may lead to convulsions and even heart failure.*

KETAMINE ('K', Special K, Vitamin K)
An anaesthetic with painkilling and hallucinogenic properties that usually comes in tablet or powder form. Vets use a similar drug to anaesthetise animals in surgery. Ketamine is a prescription only medicine. This means possession is not illegal but supply may carry Class C penalties.

The effects

- *Ketamine works by numbing physical sensation. This can leave a user unable to move and feeling somehow detached from their body.*

Hallucinations may also kick in, depending on the user's mood and environment.

The effects can lasts up to three hours.

The risks

The experience may be very alarming, and this can continue until the effects of the drug wear off.

The numbing effect of the drug means users risk serious injury without realising it.

Excessive doses can cause serious breathing problems. Users risk vomiting, unconsciousness and even heart failure. Too much can kill, but there is no such thing as a safe dose.

Ketamine can be extremely dangerous when mixed with other drugs or alcohol.

The long-term effects of recreational ketamine use are not yet fully understood.

GASES, AEROSOLS & GLUE (solvents)

Compound substances found in a range of common products, such as hair spray, lighter refills, air fresheners, tins or tubes of glue, some paint thinners and correcting fluids. Inhaling the vapours can produce a high, but it is illegal for shopkeepers to sell to under-18s if they know or suspect the product is intended for misuse.

The effects

- *When sniffed or breathed into the lungs, users feel intensely light-headed, giggly, and dreamy. The high is often compared to feeling very drunk.*

- *The effects are immediate, but quickly fade, and wear off completely within 45 minutes (without a repeat dose).*

- *Users are often left feeling drowsy. Headaches are also a common after-effect.*

The risks

- *Misusing gases, aerosols and glue can kill, even on the first go.*

- *At least one person dies every week in the UK as a result of solvent abuse.*

- *Users run a high risk of accidents when high.*

- *Long-term abuse can damage the brain, kidneys and liver.*

HEROIN (smack, gear, H, skag, junk, brown)
A painkilling drug that originates from the opium poppy and can be smoked, snorted or injected. Heroin is a Class A drug.

The effects

A small dose can create a strong sense of well-being, warmth and security.

Larger doses can cause drowsiness and loss of consciousness.

Excessive amounts can be fatal.

The risks

Heroin can be very addictive. In chronic cases, the craving for another hit can rule a user's life.

Users may wind up relying on heroin to feel normal.

Tolerance is quick to develop, which means the user needs more to get the same effect – increasing the risk of overdose.

Withdrawing from heroin can be very hard. Medical help may be required.

- *Many users do break free of the physical dependency, but it can take years to rid your mind of the need for a fix.*

over to you

Hopefully, you'll have come this far with a better understanding of how to manage your life. It might have put you in the picture about body myths or drinking laws, or opened your eyes to what others see in you. Maybe you'll flick through the pages in future, checking out drug facts against the stories you've heard. Whatever the case, only you can decide how to act upon the info and advice in here. Nobody can forbid you from sparking up a smoke or force you to use a condom for sex, but you owe it to yourself to make informed decisions based on the facts.

As for being a boy, walk away from this book with your head held high. It's all too easy to feel uncomfortable about yourself when people are so down on lads in general, but don't let your gender overshadow the fact that you're also an individual. Providing you treat yourself and other people with respect then it makes no odds if you're male or female – you'll be sure to go far.

Unzipped contacts

"I didn't make the call for a while, but I kept the number in my pocket because I knew I needed help. When I did find the courage to pick up the phone, it was such a relief to hear a friendly voice that didn't judge me but just listened."
Nathan, 14

Acne Support Group
Members receive help, advice and information on all acne issues.
PO Box 9 Newquay
Cornwall TR9 6WG
United Kingdom
www.stopspots.org

ADFAM
National helpline for families and friends of drug users, offering confidential support and information about drugs and local services.
www.adfam.org

Al Anon and Al Ateen
Help and information for anyone whose life is affected by someone else's drinking. Contact the helpline, or write to the address below for details of groups in your area.
www.hexnet.co.uk/alanon/alateen.html
Tel: 020 7403 0888

Anti Bullying Campaign
Confidential advice and information for anyone affected by bullying.
www.bullying.co.uk

Brook Advisory Centre
Free, confidential sex advice and contraception. Call for details of your local drop-in centre.
Tel: 0800 0185 023

Careline
For anyone who would like to talk to a trained counsellor about any issue that's troubling them.
Tel: 0845 122 8622
www.carelineuk.org

Childline
Trained counsellors provide advice for young people on any issue that concerns them. Calls are free and won't appear on the phone bill. You can also write to Childline.
Freepost 1111 London N1 0BR
Tel: 0800 1111

Children's Legal Centre
Independent national charity concerned with law and policy affecting children and young people.
Young people's free phone number: 0800 783 2187
www.childrenslegalcentre.com

Cruse Bereavement Care
Free confidential advice and information for anyone affected by death.
Tel: 0808 808 1677

Depression Alliance
Confidential helpline for anyone concerned or affected by depression.
www.depressionalliance.org

Drinkline
National helpline offering confidential support and advice if you're worried about your own or someone else's drinking.
Tel: 0800 917 8282

fpa
Information service on family planning and all aspects of sexual health.
Helpline: 0845 3101334

Frank
Free confidential advice, information and help about drugs. Open 24 hours a day. They can refer you on to local drug services and send out free literature.
Tel: 0800 77 66 00
www.talktofrank.com

Gamblers Anonymous
Self help groups and separate meetings for spouses, friends and families who are affected by gambling.
Tel: 020 7384 3040
www.gamblersanonymous.org.uk/

Lesbian and Gay Switchboard
24 hour information and help for anyone worried about their sexuality.
Tel: 020 7837 7324

Mind
For help, information and advice on any mental health issue.
Tel: 0845 766 0163

National Drugs Helpline also called Talk To Frank/Frank
Talk to Frank is a website and telephone helpline offering advice, information and support to anyone concerned about drugs and solvent/volatile substance misuse.
Tel (Helpline): 0800 77 66 00
Tel (Text): 0800 917 8765
Web: www.talktofrank.com

National Society for the Prevention of Cruelty to Children (NSPCC)
Confidential helpline for young people concerned about all issues of safety.
Tel: 0808 800 5000

Netdoctor
Independent UK health website, with factfiles written by doctors and medical professionals.
www.netdoctor.co.uk

Parentline Plus
Advice and information for people living in a stepfamily.
Tel: 0808 800 2222

QUITLINE
Helpline staffed by qualified counsellors. Call as often as you like, for practical help and information on giving up cigarettes.
Tel: 0800 00 22 00

Release
Advice, counselling and information, on drug health, welfare and legal issues.
Tel: 0845 4500 215

Samaritans
Confidential emotional support for any person who is suicidal or despairing.
Tel: 08457 90 90 90
www.samaritans.org.uk

TheSite.org
Online youth advice and information resource. If you're worried about any issue affecting your life, they've got it covered.
www.thesite.org

Victim Support
Support and information for victims of any kind of crime.
Tel: 0845 30 30 900
www.victimsupport.org.uk

Youth Access
Call for details of youth counselling
services in your area.
Tel: 020 8772 9900
www.youthaccess.org.uk

AUSTRALIA

Lifeline
Confidential advice.
Tel: 13 11 14 (24 hours)
www.lifeline.org.au

Kids Help Line
Telephone counselling service.
Tel: 1800 551 800 (24 hours)
www.kidshelp.com.au

Reach Out!
Website for young people.
www.reachout.com.au

Beyond Blue
Information about depression.
www.beyondblue.org.au

CANADA

Kids Help Phone
Tel: 1 800 668 6868 (24 hours)
www.kidshelpphone.ca

NEW ZEALAND

Kidsline
Tel: 0800 543754
www.kidsline.org.nz

Youthline
Tel: 0800 376633
www.youthline.co.nz

REPUBLIC OF IRELAND

Childline
Freephone 1800 666 666
www.ispcc.ir

ONE2ONE
Drugs and sexual health helpline
for young people.
Tel: (021) 427 5615

Al-Alon and Alateen
Help for families of alcoholics.
5-6 Capel Street, Dublin 1
Tel: (01) 873 2699

**Irish Society for Prevention of
Cruelty to Children**
29 Lower Baggot Street, Dublin 2
(01) 676 7960

**National Association for Victims
of Bullying**
Frederick Street, Clara, Co Offaly
Tel: (0506) 31590

Samaritans
Tel: 1850 609 090

SOUTH AFRICA

Lifeline National Helpline
Tel: 0861 322 322

Unzipped glossary

acne Skin disorder that commonly kicks in during puberty, caused by an overproduction of sebum. The resulting blockages give rise to anything from blackheads to pimples and cysts.

adolescence The stage between youth and adulthood, marked by the physical changes of puberty and also fights with your folks because they won't let you stay out as long as you like.

bisexual Term used to describe someone who is sexually attracted to both men and women.

blow job Properly known as oral sex, which means using the mouth and/or tongue to stimulate the genitals of a sexual partner. Oral sex performed on a woman is known as 'cunnilingus' and 'fellatio' when performed on a man.

B.O. Short for body odour – a naturally occurring niff caused by bacteria breaking down sweat on the surface of the skin. Hot spots include armpits and the groin area.

chromosome A naturally occurring file containing info about you, stored as a microscopic spiral within every cell in your body. All 46 chromosomes in a human cell are divided into pairs (one side from your dad, the other from your mum) and contain different data relating to stuff like appearance, resistance to disease, and your gender.

circumcision Simple operation to remove the foreskin, usually on religious grounds but in some cases for medical reasons.

clitoris Small, fleshy and highly sensitive bump found just in front of the opening of the vagina. The clitoris functions as a main source of sexual pleasure.

contraception Broad term used to describe any means of preventing pregnancy (i.e. birth control devices such as condoms or The Pill).

ejaculation Also known as 'coming', the moment of ejaculation is caused by an involuntary contraction of muscles, often at the point of orgasm, and which results in semen spurting from the tip of the penis.

epididymis Highly coiled tube which connects each testicle to the rest of the plumbing at the base of the penis. This is where sperm develop fully following their origin in the testicles. You can feel the epididymis above and behind each testicle and they are a common place to find harmless lumps and bumps (get your doc to check any lumps though, to be sure).

erection Name given to describe the penis when it's stiff as a result of sexual arousal.

foreplay Any kind of sexual activity that happens before penetration, such as kissing, hugging, stroking and/or oral sex. Inviting your partner to play a videogame doesn't count, no matter how much it turns you on.

foreskin Name for the open-ended hood of skin covering the penis head.

frenulum Sounds like a musical instrument, but actually refers to the band of skin on the underside of the penis that attaches the foreskin to the penis. It tends to be quite tight, but if it's causing you discomfort then see your GP.

glans AKA the penis head or helmet. The glans has a purplish appearance and is very sensitive to touch, particularly when you're sexually aroused.

growing pains Term used during puberty to describe minor aches and twinges, particularly in the arms and legs. There is no hard evidence to prove the common belief that growing pains are down to an increased rate in bone development. In fact, many experts suggest it's simply the result of physical exercise. If in doubt, see your doctor.

homosexual Term used to describe someone who is sexually attracted to people of the same gender.

hormones Naturally occurring chemicals that regulate physical development. During puberty, male sex hormones tend to rage through a boy's body like storm water in a sewer, but it all calms down eventually.

hot flush Feeling of warmth that can spread across the upper body and leave you feeling sweaty. Often occurs during puberty, and is believed to be caused by necessary changes in hormone levels that also happen to mess with the body's temperature controls.

hymen Thin membrane found inside the opening of the vagina. Often breaks on first intercourse and can cause slight bleeding. It's very fragile, however, and sometimes breaks long before as a result of sporting activity or use of tampons.

intercourse Another word for sex (which is often called 'sexual intercourse'), in which the penis enters the vagina.

masturbation The act of stimulating the sexual organs for pleasure. Often viewed as a teen boy's favourite hobby, but it's by no means compulsory and nor will it make you blind/sick/insane etc.

orgasm The peak of sexual pleasure, for both women and men. Continued stimulation may also result in further orgasms for women, while men require a recovery period – often characterised by a need for sleep or pizza.

periods Part of a woman's 'menstrual cycle' that describes the monthly bleeding from the womb, which passes out through the vagina. It's perfectly natural, and a sign that the female body is fertile. Periods are also something boys need to know about to avoid accusations of being 'a typical man'.

premature ejaculation A condition that means you come (ejaculate) during sex before you or your partner feel ready. Premature ejaculation among young men is often remedied with simple exercises and/or sexual experience (see pp87–88).

puberty A stage of physical changes during adolescence, controlled by hormones, that results in boys and girls maturing sexually. It's marked by physical changes such as a deepening voice, development of sexual organs and body hair, while the way you feel about yourself becomes more complex.

scrotum Another word for the sack that contains your balls. This can hang down in hot weather like an overstretched carrier bag, or bunch up tight when it's cold.

sebum Oily secretion designed to keep the skin supple.

semen Milky white fluid, often thin, sometimes thick and/or lumpy, which is ejaculated from the penis on orgasm. Semen contains sperm and other fluids. The volume produced in a normal amount of 'come' is anywhere between 1.5 and 5mls – which is roughly a teaspoonful in volume.

sperm Tadpole-type male sex cells designed to connect with the female egg and fertilise it. About 50 million sperm are present in a typical 'serving' of semen.

testicles Spherical structures housed inside the sack that hangs underneath your penis, and generally known as 'balls'. Medics also call them 'testes'. The testicles produce sperm, and should be checked on a regular basis for any unusual lumps or bumps (see checking for testicular cancer pp32–33).

testosterone The male sex hormone, responsible for the physical characteristics that make up a man.

urethra Tube that runs to the end of the penis, allowing urine to exit as well as semen on ejaculation – but not at the same time.

vagina Part of a woman's sex organs. It's the muscular passage leading from the neck of the womb (cervix) to the opening of the vulva. The vagina is basically what the penis penetrates during sex.

virility A word often used in macho terms to describe your ability to perform as a lover. Virility isn't something that can be measured, however, and nor should sex be an act that requires marks out of ten.

wet dream The release of semen during sleep. It's perfectly natural, and your body's way of checking that everything is functioning sexually. It doesn't necessarily mean you've been dreaming about sex, and tends to stop after adolescence.

index